International

Relations

– For People Who Hate Politics

An Introduction to the Causes of
Conflict and Cooperation Between States.

By Albert Rutherford

Co-authored and revised by

Zoe McKey

Printed in the United States of America.

First Printing, 2022

ISBN 9798839934924

www.albertrutherford.com

albertrutherfordbooks@gmail.com

Deepen your understanding of the world with these complimentary gifts.

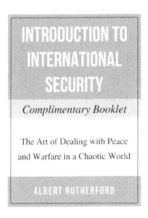

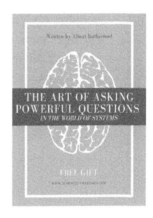

Thank you for choosing my book, International Relations – For People Who Hate Politics! I would like to show my appreciation by giving you two booklets, The Art of Asking Powerful Questions – in the World of Systems and Introduction to International Security.

The Art of Asking Powerful Questions will cover:

- What bounded rationality is,
- How to distinguish event- and behavior-level analysis,
- How to find optimal leverage points,
- And how to ask powerful questions using a systems thinking perspective.

Introduction to International Security will include:

- The difference between strategic and security studies,
- The three paradigms of security,
- The key assumptions of security,
- And how security is defined on the international field.

Visit www.albertrutherford.com to download the two booklets.

If you're having any difficulties downloading the files, please contact me at albertrutherfordbooks@gmail.com and I will remedy the issue.

Table of Contents

A special thanks to Zoe McKey, who offered me her guidance and expertise

during the writing of this book.

Introduction

"Oh, those sleazy politicians!"

"Which is the only mammal that can thrive without a backbone? A politician!"

"How can you spot a politician lying? Their mouth is moving."

Have you ever encountered any of these remarks or jokes during your lifetime? If you live on planet Earth, you probably have. Disdain for politicians is just as common as for the parking enforcers. Politicians represent not only a country, a county, or a smaller community – they also represent the art of politics. In the minds of many, politics and politicians became synonyms. But is it prudent to judge a field of science based on some of its representatives? For instance, if you encountered a bad doctor, would it mean that medical science itself is useless?

"But what if all doctors were bad? Would theoretical medicine matter if all its practitioners did a poor job?" one might ask. That's a tricky question – and if this was true, if all medical professionals were as good as dart throwing monkeys, then sure, theoretical medicine wouldn't serve us much. But that's an extreme statement and an incorrect one. By the same token, not all politicians are sleazy, lying, backbone lacking individuals. I would go as far as to say, most of them are not. If you're reading this book, there is a high chance you live in a country with democratic values. One of these values is the privilege to vote. Each citizen, therefore, who can legally vote is a shaper of their country's politics. Ordinary citizens don't need to be politicians by profession to contribute meaningfully …

Sticking to the medical analogy, not all patients have to be doctors, but knowing the basics of how the human body works – how certain types of foods, a lack of exercise and sleep, stress affect them – will make them make better choices and be healthier individuals. Magnify this to the nation level, and you get a healthier, more mindful and prosperous society. Similarly, knowing the basics of political science will help voters make better, more informed decisions. Spread this thought to the state level, and you'll get a more educated and intentional society.

Politicians are not "rotten" because politics are derived from the devil. It's the other way around. Partially, society breeds people with values that are not always focused on the common good, and partially, it is human nature to take as much as one can until hitting a socially imposed barrier. If some individuals behave in dislikeable ways, it is because – at the end of the day

– they can. It's not the fault of the individual; the problem lies within the system. "Well, let's just change the system, then!" one might think. Agreed, but by their nature, systems are slow and hard to change. A system is an abstract concept – the result of elements interacting with one another in pursuit of a purpose. In our case, the political system at its most basic level is comprised of a country's citizens who interact a certain way.

A meaningful change to the system has to start with a shift in the mindset of its smallest components – the everyday folk. You and me. The first step is to separate political science as a field of study from its demonized earthly representatives. Hating politics and digging one's head in the sand, avoiding voting, or voting for whoever offers a bigger hot-dog during the campaign period is not an informed and empowered way of exercising one's privileges. Practicing such a behavior on a country level leads to undesirable results. How can we avoid this?

One word: education. Learning about the programs and the individuals involved in political campaigns is a good practice. But it's not enough. We, as a society, need to know and understand the contextual framework or paradigm in which these actors operate. We need to understand the basics of politics. Knowledge doesn't only serve a better decision-making potential. It also makes people feel more empowered and more likely to go to the voting booths.[iii] There are many other variables that affect voter turnout and satisfaction, of course, such as age, socioeconomic status, accessibility to vote, and others. Some of these factors are outside an individual's immediate control. What one can do, and no one can ever take away from them, is what they learn. Becoming as educated on basic political matters as possible is never a bad idea. And thanks to the internet, a lot of knowledge is at our fingertips.

There was a time when politics was synonymous with positive concepts, such as accountability, deliberation, intentionality, and public scrutiny. Today that's barely the case. I will not lie. You reading this – or any similar - book will not change much about the system. But it may change how you think about politics and how you exercise your political power. You may share your knowledge with your friends, who will also read this – or a similar – book and change their ways. And they will share it with two of their friends. The power of exponential growth will slowly but surely create a shift in society.

In this book, I will talk about the field of study that could be considered the backbone of contemporary political dynamics, international relations. Today, the world is more interconnected than ever. Your choices as a voting citizen not only affect the affairs of your own country but also you have an impact on global dynamics – no pressure. This read will help you understand:

- how global politics came into being,

- who its main influencers were,

- what the leading ideological concepts throughout its existence were.

In the following pages, I will provide the groundwork for international politics. This is not only a fun, informative read but also a solid primer for understanding some key political concepts. What does it mean to have a constructivist approach to politics? What's the difference between Marxism, socialism, and communism? How do international politics and political science, in general, adapt to a changing world?

Find out the answers to all these questions and much more in International Relations- For People Who Hate Politics. I invite you on a thousand-mile and thousand-year journey. Come, join me.

Part I

Foundations of International Relations

- Historical Background
- Theoretical Background

Historical Background

Chapter 1: Greece and the Work of Thucydides

Thucydides was among the first western historians to chronicle a major conflict using scientific standards of impartiality. He wrote a historical account of the Peloponnesian War through evidence gathering and cause and effect analysis – a revolutionary feat at a time when crowd-pleasing stories involving religious explanations for events were the norm. Instead, Thucydides analyzed the human factors and motivations that led to and amplified the Peloponnesian War, a conflict that occurred during his lifetime.

The Peloponnesian War was fought between the Delian League led by Athens and the Peloponnesian League led by Sparta from 431 to 404 BC (Chairil, 2013).[iii] When writing *History of the Peloponnesian War*, Thucydides relied on interpretations of chronological facts.

He primarily employed eyewitness accounts, evaluations of sources, and his own experience to recount the events leading to the breakout of the war and the ones that followed. The first book sought to explain the reasons behind the outbreak of the Peloponnesian War, and books 2 through 8 focused on the war itself (Chairil, 2013).[iv] Throughout the book, Thucydides utilized analyses of human factors and motivations driving the war. In the first book, Thucydides argued the Spartans were "compelled" to war, suggesting they had no choice but to combat Athens' rising power (Morley, 2020)[v]. To support his claim, he laid out the perceived causes of the war, focusing primarily on economic and conflicting political power struggles as the leading causes.

The Delian League, which started as a small group of city-states following the end of the Persian Wars, was developing into a significant power in the Mediterranean region decades before the Peloponnesian War (Chairil, 2013).[vi] As Athens grew stronger, it began to dominate other city-states, subjugating them to tribute-paying subject states to the Delian League (Chairil, 2013).[vii] Part of the Peloponnesian League, Sparta was particularly fearful of Athens' growing influence in the ancient Greek world. Several events played a role in increasing tensions, including, but not limited to, Sparta dismissing the Athenian force after summoning it to help suppress a rebellion on Spartan territory (Chairil, 2013).[viii]

While Athens and Sparta fought together against the Persians from 492 to 449 BC, Athens renounced its alliance with Sparta during the Helot revolt (Chairil, 2013).[ix] During that time, Greek city-states placed far more emphasis on local loyalties than on their shared cultural heritage. Nevertheless, the cultural considerations within Thucydides' writings were paramount because they explained how alliance politics played an essential role in the outbreak of the war. Alliances moved from being formed to counter attacks on a large part of the ancient Greek world to being founded based on regional fidelities.

It was only a matter of time until the Delian and Peloponnesian Leagues collided. The Delian League's power was augmented by its naval superiority, used to intimidate allies. The Peloponnesian League, headed by Sparta, grew increasingly concerned about Athens' ability to dominate the seas. Sparta and Athens supervised different spheres of influence, but Sparta regarded Athens' rapid rise as an empire as a great threat to the traditional balance of power. By maintaining that war is likely, if not inevitable, when a rising power confronts another power to protect its interests, Thucydides established a foundational international relations (IR) theory that came to be known as the Thucydides Trap. His contribution to the study of IR founded the core realist assumptions surrounding the balance of power, security dilemma, and morality in a perceived state of permanent anarchy. We'll learn about these concepts in detail in the following chapters.

Thucydides' Enduring Influence on the Study of International Relations

Thucydides' contributions to the study of international relations have secured him a place among the forefathers of the realist school of thought. While Thucydides was alive more than 2,000 years ago, scholars still heavily rely on his work to make sense of modern international politics (Morley, 2020).[x] Most notably, the Thucydides Trap theory is broadly employed to explain power dynamics at the international level. The Thucydides Trap is effectively a dilemma that a dominant power faces when a rising power threatens its authority. By linking human nature to the nature of war in his writings, Thucydides determines that all wars have some intrinsic features relevant across conflicts throughout time.

Furthermore, some scholars, particularly those within the realist school of thought, have interpreted Thucydides' Melian Dialogue to mean only practical considerations count in international politics, not morality or ethics (Morley, 2020).[xi]

Years into the Peloponnesian War, Athens demanded the neutral island of Melos to join the war on the side of the Delian League. The Melians, people more closely related to the Spartans, argued the law of nations protected their neutral status and no nation had the right to attack another without being provoked (Debnar,

2017).[xii] American international political scholar Robert Keohane has pointed to three main assumptions laid out in Thucydides' writings: states are the key units of action (1) that largely behave rationally as they seek power (2) either as an end in itself or as a means to other ends (3).[xiii] This suggests that, in acting rationally, states often set questions of morality aside, as illustrated in the Melian Dialogue. And if states behave rationally, then their behavior can be understood and assessed.

According to some IR scholars, there have been at least sixteen cases when a rising power confronted an established power in the last five hundred years, and twelve of those cases resulted in war.[xiv] Because Thucydides' works included timeless observations, scholars have employed his frameworks to understand numerous historical and modern-day conflicts, including the current relationship between the United States and China (Morley, 2020).[xv] At first glance, the contentious relationship between the United States and China looks like the one between Sparta and Athens that Thucydides meticulously fleshed out in his writings. In recent decades, China has developed into an international economic powerhouse with the ability to challenge the global status quo. And it is no secret that China seeks to solidify its own sphere of influence, since it has repeatedly announced its goals of advancing global multipolarity (CBS News, 2022).[xvi] However, various academics have questioned the extent to which Thucydides' theories can be utilized in an increasingly interdependent world. Some have even argued that an all-out conflict between the U.S. and China was unlikely due to their closely integrated economies (Morley, 2020).[xvii] Scholars have also analogized the tensions between Sparta and Athens to make sense of the Cold War dynamic, even though the United States and the Soviet Union do not fit the same characterizations of Athens and Sparta that Thucydides wrote about two thousand years ago (Morley, 2020).[xviii]

Nevertheless, Thucydides' discourse on human nature simplified the process of assessing conflicts. Though Thucydides did not establish the principles of international politics outright, scholars have extrapolated universal norms from his texts. In *Thucydides and International Relations*, Professor Neville Morley explains IR scholars must not overlook assessments of Thucydides' works and their implications because they prompt theorists to consider connections between the past and present (Morley, 2020).[xix] His works remain relevant because they encourage further discussion on the foundations of war and illustrate the consequences of pursuing power as a policy tool.

How Thucydides' Models Can Be Employed Beyond Traditional IR Frameworks.

Over time, however, IR academics have questioned the extent to which Thucydides' History of the Peloponnesian War can be explored through a realist or neo-realist perspective. Thucydides carefully outlined the causes of the Peloponnesian War by describing the motivations and alliances of the involved parties. Thus, he painted a highly complex, multi-layered picture of all facets of the war. Realists regard Thucydides as the first writer in the realist tradition, but some scholars have argued that compartmentalizing Thucydides' perspective within one school of thought is counterproductive (Bagby, 1994).[xx] Although Thucydides' pessimistic observations of human nature overlap with those of classical realism, his thorough explanations of cultural differences and their influence on decision-making provide an alternative to black and white assessments (Badby, 1994).[xxi]

In *The Use and Abuse of Thucydides in International Relations*, Professor Bagby argues the Thucydidean perspective strays from the core assumptions of political realism because it does not always treat states as primary actors, and it does not show that states constantly seek to maximize their power (Bagby, 1994).[xxii] Consequently, Thucydides explores individual and national character, moral distinctions, and political rhetoric to explain state actions, veering from simplistic power distribution analyses (Bagby, 1994).[xxiii]

Thucydides' relevance rests primarily on the complexity of his observations that boil down to the essence of humanity. In the *History of the Peloponnesian War*, he explores how the interplay of human nature in conflict scenarios can affect outcomes. Professor Bagby contends

Thucydides' approach to dissecting the causes and effects of war requires us to reject relying on any one IR theory (Bagby, 1994).[xxiv] Thucydides omitted his personal beliefs from his texts, opting instead to create a work that could be useful to future generations. Unfortunately, the post-World War II era has also been plagued by various conflicts, and to make sense of ongoing wars, scholars still rely on the classics.

Thucydides' works provide scholars with a framework to challenge existing structures by prompting them to analyze state behavior from a fundamental human level. Transcending space and time, his writings can help this generation better understand the implications of human nature concerning war by giving us the tools to assess variables, such as culture, speech, and morals, which are aspects that go beyond the dichotomy of power politics. Likewise, Thucydides' models offer ample opportunities to dissect comparable situations.

Chapter 2: Peace of Westphalia

The Peace of Westphalia followed one of the longest and most devastating conflicts in modern history. The culmination of clashes between Protestants and Catholics over the authority of the Catholic Church coupled with European power politics at the time resulted in a series of wars fought mainly in Central Europe between 1618 and 1648, known as the Thirty Years' War. During the 16th century, the Protestant Reformation divided the Holy Roman Empire. In 1555, the Peace of Augsburg attempted to settle the conflicts resulting from the religious divide by allowing rulers to choose between Roman Catholicism or Lutheranism in their respective territories. However, the many Calvinist rulers and their citizens were not recognized, resulting in tensions that caused Catholic and Protestant states to form alliances.

Ferdinand II was a devout Catholic who took power in 1617 as the King of Bohemia (today a territory of the Czech Republic) and then as the Holy Roman Emperor. Soon after rising to power, Ferdinand II revoked Emperor Rudolf II's[1] 1609 Letter of Majesty granting Protestants religious tolerance in Bohemia (Mason, 2020).[xxv] A civil war erupted in 1618 between German members of the Holy Roman Empire in response to Ferdinand II's decision to revoke religious tolerance in Bohemia. Protestants attacked Ferdinand II's palace, throwing two of his ministers out a window and forcing the Catholic King out (International Relations, 2013).[xxvi] But the Thirty Years' War was not only caused by religious struggles. Foreign powers also had a vested interest in these developments. France, Sweden, Denmark, and England offered their support to the Protestant princes of Germany fighting the Catholic Habsburgs, later backed by Spain (Patton, 2019).[xxvii] The Thirty Years' War had a profound impact on Europe's political and social landscape, claiming the lives of 4 to 12 million people and diminishing Europe's total

---

[1] Emperor of the Holy Roman Empire, King of Hungary and Croatia, King of Bohemia and Archduke of Austria between 12 October 1576 – 20 January 1612.

population by an estimated 20 percent (Daudin, 2017).[xxviii] The Holy Roman Empire alone lost about a third of its population (Patton, 2019).[xxix]

The Thirty Years' War finally ended with a series of peace treaties, namely the Treaty of Osnabrück and the Treaty of Münster, signed in 1648. Negotiations started in 1642 with diplomatic representatives from 96 separate entities meeting in the cities of Osnabrück and Münster, although some scholars argue that comprehensive negotiations that truly intended to stop wars did not begin until 1945, with the ratification of the charter of the United Nations. Intense devastation and the immense loss of life forced the concerned parties, each with their own set of goals, to the negotiation table. The peace settlement led to several territorial adjustments, including, but not limited to, the independence of the United Provinces from the Holy Roman Empire and Spain, Dutch independence from Spain, and Swedish control over the Baltic (Patton, 2019).[xxx]

The Heritage of Westphalia

The immediate impact of this historic settlement cannot be overlooked, as it involved a consorted, international diplomatic effort at a level not seen before that time that established the concept of diplomacy and negotiation. This effort led to the formal recognition of freedom of conscience, and it solidified the foundation of religious tolerance in granting Catholics and Protestants the freedom to practice their religions (International Relations, 2013).[xxxi] It also established the notion of state sovereignty by substantially increasing the power of provincial princes while reducing that of the Holy Roman Emperor.

The Peace of Westphalia fundamentally changed how the world was organized by creating a framework for modern international relations based on a realist understanding of the international system's dynamics. A constant state of conflict brought about by concepts of divinely sanctioned authority and power struggles between kingdom and religion inspired the pursuit of a more effective system of relations for states (Patton, 2019).[xxxii] The Westphalian model denounced the rule of one universal authority by recognizing that each nation state had control over its territory; thus, rulers had the power to define religion in their respective territories. The treaties essentially required its signatories to "ignore any objection made on the basis of religious supremacy," replacing the Christian community's role of states with a rule of "state consent" (Patton, 2019).[xxxiii] This revolutionary principle empowered states to engage in diplomacy with one another by establishing a norm of non-intervention in the affairs of other states. Consequently, the replacement of the Holy Roman Empire and Papacy as the supreme authority in Europe introduced the nation state as the highest authority. Without an overall authority directing regional and international policy, states were forced into a balancing act to adhere to the Westphalian model. Alliance policies became essential to prevent the domination of one specific entity, since states became regarded as equal and autonomous.

The concepts enshrined by the Peace of Westphalia paved the way for modern international norms. The Westphalian framework was adopted by various international organizations, such as the United Nations, European Union, and even the United States, to some extent, as a means to manage power. The

United Nations' predecessor, the League of Nations, adopted various Westphalian norms, including equal state sovereignty, non-intervention, and peacekeeping. It is important to highlight that the League of Nations charter employed a similar language as the Treaty of Münster in trying to ban recourse to arms for territorial expansion (Patton, 2019).[xxxiv] In *The Peace of Westphalia and its Affects on International Relations, Diplomacy and Foreign Policy*, Steve Patton refers to the compromises reached by European states as "precedents of common and international law until World War I," while arguing those precedents continued to be fundamental to the core of foreign policy (Patton, 2019).[xxxv]

The Weaknesses of the Westphalian Model

Other scholars, like Ove Bring, have pointed to the Westphalian model's weaknesses post-1648. In The Westphalian Peace Tradition in International Law, Ove Bring argued that, while the Westphalian peace and security system constructed a basis for common legal rules of coexistence, it contained no mechanisms for "implementing crisis management procedures" (Bring, 2000).[xxxvi] Part of the issue with the Westphalian peace was its inability to contain the expansion of sovereign states (International Relations, 2013).[xxxvii] The Peace of Westphalia did not result in lasting peace in Europe or elsewhere since European expansionism was not curbed by the treaties. Nevertheless, the concept of state sovereignty was further developed in the post-World War II period with decolonization efforts through independence movements. The post-World War II Era built on the Westphalian model by expanding the modern state system while simultaneously placing limitations on the behavior of states that had become challenged by supranational organizations.

Even though 1648 is considered by many IR scholars as a pillar moment when the modern international political phenomenon developed, it is crucial to highlight that the study of past developments in understanding the present is often carried out through the lens of the present moment. Scholars have embraced different interpretations of the influence of the

Westphalian system on the trajectory of world politics since 1648. Some scholars have regarded the Peace of Westphalia as a paradigm shift in how the modern state system developed (Beaulac, 2004).[xxxviii]

In *Perspectives on Sovereignty in the Current Context: A Canadian Viewpoint*, Canadian scholar Donat Pharand contended the notion of state sovereignty as described by the Peace of Westphalia became an established principle of international law (Pharand, 1994).[xxxix] However, various critics have pointed out that the Westphalian peace is a myth. Related scholarship suggests the Peace of Westphalia was not the modern world order's starting point but rather a comfortable starting position for international relations scholars to explain IR frameworks by using generally accepted history. Critics of the Westphalian myth often base their arguments on textual and post-Westphalian peace historical analyses. Law professor Stéphane Beaulac argues the universal authority of the Pope and Holy Roman Emperor was "severely depleted" by the Reformation and the centralization of government before the Thirty Years' War broke out (Beaulac, 2004).[xl] In turn, states did not seek a peace settlement to establish equal sovereignty but rather to end the war and exploit the Empire's weaknesses for personal gain. In turn, the international system continued operating in line with a hierarchical model, rather than one of sovereign equality. Further, Beaulac highlights that the Westphalian state system was a continuation of the processes in place, which did not reconstruct multilayered ruling in Europe but merely allowed separate entities to "claim more authority through enhanced independence" (Beaulac, 2004).[xli] Hence, the Peace of Westphalia implicitly, rather than explicitly, recognized the principle of sovereign equality because it did not mention the question of sovereignty outright (International Relations, 2013).[xlii]

According to this argument, the Peace of Westphalia did not amount to a revolutionary shift in how the international system was organized. Nor was it effective at staving off future conflicts, as some theorists have argued, due to the weakening unity of the Holy Roman Empire through the emergence of somewhat uncontrollable separate polities with varying domestic and foreign policy goals (Zurbuchen, 2019).[xliii] The treaties incorporated clauses that allowed newly formed sovereign entities to intervene should the Holy Roman Empire break the treaties, which seriously challenges the Westphalian legacy of establishing the principle of sovereignty (International Relations, 2013). [xliv]

The Peace of Westphalia is undoubtedly significant within the study of international relations. It marked the end of the last great religious war in Europe, as well as the beginning of a period of political transition. However, the extent to which the Peace of Westphalia marked an unprecedented change in the international system's organization, rather than a continuation of the status quo, remains a valid point of inquiry. Relying solely on the Westphalian model in the 21st century to explain international relations may prove to be disadvantageous and shortsighted. Current global challenges transcend borders and hierarchies of governmental organizations. The interconnectivity of the current world order perpetuated by the rise of supranational organizations is rocking the Westphalian foundations of the state system by weakening the idea of sovereignty as we know it.

Chapter 3: Impact of World War I on the Study of International Relations.

World War I marked the first time the world was truly embroiled in a conflict that spanned continents. The assassination of Archduke Franz Ferdinand of Austria-Hungary was the immediate cause of the Great War, but appropriating its origin to one single moment in history is counterfactual and unproductive. The fundamental source of World War One is complex, involving the actions of numerous nations. Some scholars have primarily blamed Germany by arguing it had secret ambitions to annex a large part of Europe (Cameron, 2014).[xlv] Others have claimed Germany failed to put pressure on its ally, Austria-Hungary, to stop the outbreak of the war, and some scholars even credit Great Britain for escalating the war by getting involved (Cameron, 2014).[xlvi] The causes of the Great War can be traced back to the late 1800s, when Europe became increasingly polarized through various realignments and alliance formations. World War I is considered by many to be one of the most important political events in history because of its remarkable impact on the modern global system (Wisidagama, 2017).[xlvii] For perhaps the first time in history, the Great War's profound human cost prompted a cohesive, global pursuit to make sense of the driving forces behind the war to evade future conflicts. Over 16 million people died, and the war wiped away an entire generation of men (Cameron, 2014).[xlviii]

The immediate aftermath of World War I saw new developments arise across various fields and industries. WW I changed the nature of warfare with technological advancements taking center stage in conflicts that followed. It reconstructed Europe's class structure by speeding up the decline of the upper class through greater political representation for the masses (Cameron, 2014).[xlix] Social and political changes brought about by the war democratized international political theory and discourse.

Greater openness was fostered by scrutiny of the elites' ability to resolve conflicts peacefully, which faltered in the war's run-up. The notion that an enlightened and well-informed public was a prerequisite to global peace gained traction, and the establishment of world affairs councils, international relations curricula, and schools of thought soon followed (Pfaltzgraff JR.).[l]

The realization that an educated, peace-seeking populace could help prevent major conflicts compelled nations to look inward. The paradox of the United States sending 200,000 Black soldiers to Europe during World War I to fight for freedom and democracy during the segregationist Jim Crow era prompted the formation of new campaigns and organizations that actively fought discrimination as a means to elevate the positions of underrepresented citizens (Mock, 2018).[li] In other areas of the world, the dissolution of empires paved the way for nationalism and self-determination. For example, in the Middle East, European powers extended colonial rule over the region following the collapse of the Ottoman Empire (Mock, 2018).[lii] So while World War I encouraged freedom movements for underrepresented and oppressed populations in America, these movements became inherently nationalistic in the Middle East. Thus, questions rose surrounding how democratic institutions based on mutual norms could succeed globally when the war triggered different social changes among countries.

In *World War 1 and IR Theory*, Professor Pfaltzgraff credits the forces unleashed by World War I as a primary driver of developing IR theories that later sought to eliminate or pacify global issues, such as nuclear proliferation, information warfare, and terrorism (Pfaltzgraff JR.).[liii] It became clear after the Great War that the 19th-century nation-state system was ineffective at preserving the balance of power to avoid war. The realist school of thought ascribed the war's outbreak to balance of power disruptions and/or fears of imbalances primarily on the part of the Germans. The liberal school of thought's explanations focus more on diplomatic failures, the breakdown of civil institutions within Germany, and the world's unreadiness to welcome liberal principles, like international trade and conflict resolution. Regardless of the different diagnostic approaches, the two leading IR schools of thought became primarily concerned with conceptualizing new global management systems in the period after World War I.

Different schools of thought were also born and amplified by the liberal and realist schools' observed weaknesses in explaining certain phenomena. Constructivism became a well-respected school of thought because it offered explanations beyond the bounds of traditional frameworks. At the time, this relatively new theory emphasized the study of social factors in context. Constructivism better compliments liberal methods of international relations because of its emphasis on how collective interests can become international interests. If the collective believes in peaceful conflict resolution, then the global sphere's priorities can change accordingly (Pfaltzgraff JR.).[liv] The growing openness to adopting new theoretical structures accelerated the development of international relations as an academic field of study.

Implications of America's Rise to Power for International Relations

The United States generally favored non-interventionism prior to and for some time after World War I, but after arriving in Europe in 1917, American forces helped turn the tide of the war (Hindley, 2017).[lv] The end of the Great War saw the emergence of the U.S. as a world power that became involved in developing the League of Nations Covenant, the first global intergovernmental organization with a mission to preserve peace (Pfaltzgraff JR.).[lvi] The U.S. conceived its newfound role in the international sphere as a liberal one (Mock, 2018).[lvii] Yet, racial injustices contradicted the United States' newfound position as a champion for liberty.

Nevertheless, the United States' economic and military power was augmented during World War I, raising it to a global power status. It wasn't until the aftermath of World War II that the U.S., a new global power, ventured to create a post-war liberal order (Pfaltzgraff JR.).[lviii] This signaled a new approach to international relations, one that emphasized peace through strength, human rights and representation, and the growth of international organizations (Pfaltzgraff JR).[lix]

These developments emerged as a reaction to both world wars. However, the events leading up to and during World War I and II were analyzed and addressed by the liberal world order's founders through a Eurocentric lens. This disparity encouraged a search for knowledge riddled with sociological and contextual complexities. These complexities gave rise to the study of international relations as an academic discipline with the ultimate goal of analyzing and combining theories to understand contemporary problems comprehensively so they can be resolved before they escalate.

International Relations as a Field of Study

International relations is a relatively young field of study, born out of the traumatic experience of World War I and evolving to reflect the changing global order following World War II.[lx] International relations is considered a discipline because it includes multiple theories, concepts, and research methodologies to analyze distinct subject matters that have developed over time (Why is International Relations a discipline?, 2019).[lxi]

The study of IR can be traced back to the historical writings of Thucydides during the fifth century BC. However, it was not until 1648, with the Peace of Westphalia, that IR developed to incorporate a modern framework of study. The Peace of Westphalia created a structure that supported the global order until the onset of World War I. Incorporating nationalistic principles that formalized the idea of national sovereignty, The Peace of Westphalia created the foundation for the development of the modern nation-state system (Wisidagama, 2017).[lxii] Therefore, the primary driver of international relations from the middle of the 17th century to the beginning of the 20th century was the nation state acting to achieve its national interest, often resulting in war (Wisidagama, 2017).[lxiii] The end of World War I rendered the balance of power system obsolete. Still, the disaster it caused made the study of international relations popular among ordinary citizens instead of just politicians and diplomats.

In the period between the two world wars, international relations as an academic discipline focused on political and diplomatic relations, and its study was approached through idealistic principles (Wisidagama, 2017).[lxiv] In turn, the League of Nations was created to replace the former balance of power system. The League of Nations set parameters for global cooperation to maintain peace, but it ultimately failed due to its idealistic nature.

Following the end of World War II, international relations as an academic discipline advanced to include the study of emerging issues, like terrorism, energy, and globalization. Further, IR is now also concerned with studying non-state actors, like international or non-governmental organizations, whereas it was primarily concerned with state power plays before World War I. World War II created an urgency for developing a new global order, so understanding the many facets of society became a requirement for preserving peace. Modern developments facilitated the amelioration of international relations by encouraging scientific analyses of the causes and effects of war (Wisidagama, 2017).[lxv] Finally, increasing interconnectivity decreased the chance of circumventing externalities caused by global events. International relations thus became an academic discipline rather than a mere field of study because new theories and concepts were created to understand the effect of technological advancements, interdependence, and emerging systems within the global order.

Chapter 4: The Cold War and International Relations

World War II transformed the once allied United States and the Soviet Union into world powers. Ideological differences and political rivalry between the two superpowers would mark the beginning of the Cold War, a conflict that lasted more than four decades.

Because World War II had a devastating impact on the European continent, American President Truman devised the Marshall Plan to aid Europe's economic and social recovery. Enacted in 1948, the Marshall Plan provided more than $15 billion in aid to help rebuild Western Europe.[lxvi] The Soviet Union saw the Marshall Plan as an American tool for intervening in countries' domestic affairs, thus choosing not to join the plan and further propelling the two powers into chilling tensions. The Soviet Union had some valid reasons for distrusting the United States. President Truman had taken a hardline stance against Stalin, and western politicians employed anti-communist hysteria to amplify their influence (Naranjo, 2018).[lxvii] The CIA further aided western interests by reportedly supporting anti-communist uprisings in places like Ukraine.[lxviii] Mistrust and the Soviet Union's refusal to participate in the Marshall Plan established competing spheres of influence, which set the stage for the Cold War.[lxix]

With U.S.-Soviet relations at an all-time low, American officials adopted a policy of containment against the Soviet threat. The policy was aimed at containing a Soviet expansion of socialist influence and power. To restrain the Soviet Union's sphere of influence, the United States supported corrupt, anti-democratic governments that were friendly to America, and the Soviet Union responded by subsidizing groups that were favorable to their own global interests (Naranjo, 2018).[lxx] America's policy of containment, however, provided a rationale for an arms buildup that was met with a Soviet response in kind. Both powers pursued the development of sophisticated weaponry and nuclear weapons, but they withheld from using them. Instead, the United States and the Soviet Union chose to assert their power by using countries who did not possess weapons of mass destruction to engage in proxy wars.[lxxi]

Cold War Era Proxy Wars

Before the Cold War, most third world countries were under colonial control, and freedom movements prompted a need for financial and military aid.[lxxii] America and the Soviet Union capitalized on the emergence of new states by funding and supporting ideological allies. During the Cold War, the United States and the Soviet Union indirectly engaged in numerous armed conflicts, with more notable ones being the Korean and Vietnam wars. The Korean War, for example, was perpetuated by Soviet support for North Korea and American support for South Korea. A similar trend can be seen in the Vietnam War, where American President Kennedy approved a military campaign to aid Vietnam's nationalist government because he was convinced the

Soviet Union was aiding the northern communists, militarily and financially.

Realizing they had to garner support from third world governments to maintain and expand their influence, the United States and the Soviet Union began supporting insurgent groups to undermine unsupportive governments.[lxxiii] America supported anti-communist factions in countries such as Angola, Namibia, and Nicaragua, while the Soviet Union aided their socialist counterparts and engaged in crushing anti-communist uprisings throughout Eastern Europe. Furthermore, the indirect infighting between America and the Soviet Union proved to have a dire impact on the Middle East. While both America and the Soviet Union supported the creation of the state of Israel, which was able to defeat a number of anti-Zionist attacks due to support from the two world powers, Soviet sentiments surrounding Israel changed during the 1960s, prompting the socialist power to redirect its support toward Arab countries.[lxxiv] Cold War-era alliances in the Middle East incited proxy conflicts between Israel and Arab states, providing a foundation for ongoing conflicts in the region.

The Cold War's Effect on International Relations

During the Cold War, two ideologies permeated global relations, dividing the world into three spheres. The western sphere of influence consisted of democratic countries, the eastern sphere was made up of countries with communist governments, and the non-aligned camp included neutral states (The Cold War: International Relations between 1945 and 1989, 2020).[lxxv] Ideological alliances led to the formation of NATO and the Warsaw Pact. The two world powers sought to safeguard and enlarge their respective alliances through nuclear proliferation. The arms race reached a critical point during the Cuban Missile Crisis, putting the world on the cusp of nuclear war. At the same time, a policy of mutually assured destruction was formulated to restrain the use of nuclear warheads. The Soviet Union and the United States never engaged in a nuclear conflict, opting instead to manipulate world affairs through alliance systems and proxy wars.

The Cold War had an immense impact on international relations. To understand how the Cold War shaped the global sphere, realist theory was heavily employed because it simplified the understanding of power dynamics between states.[lxxvi] Although realists disagreed about the level of danger a bipolar world posed, they concluded that states would always seek ways to survive absent a central authority.[lxxvii]

In 1989, the Soviet Union collapsed, and the Cold War ended. Fears of mutually assured destruction and an economic downturn prompted the Soviet Union to pursue some form of international cooperation. Disarmament agreements and Gorbachev's policies of restructuring and openness ultimately led to the Union's fall that created 15 new, independent states.[lxxviii] But the emergence of the United States as the global hegemon and the changing nature of international relations created new conflicts and modes of resolution for decades to come.

The Post-Cold War Era and International Relations

The post-Cold War era, in a way, signaled the beginning of American hegemony and the installation of a new global policeman. Middle Eastern tensions that mounted during the Cold War resulted in an American foothold in the region. In Asia, U.S. foreign policy became one of stabilization, and elsewhere, the United States sought to balance tensions through military and diplomatic coalitions. America's influence over how international relations were conducted after the Cold War cannot be overstated. However, multipolarity can also describe international relations after 1989. At least five major powers, namely the United States, Europe, China, Japan, and Russia, dominated international affairs, albeit in different ways (Yilmaz, 2008).[lxxix] Due to the interconnected nature of the post-cold war international arena, major powers have been impelled toward cooperation. Simultaneously, principles of cooperation were embraced after the two world wars, so the post-Cold War order could be described as the culmination of the interlinked order that followed World War Two.

Major power cooperation and enhanced forms of a collective political agency have fashioned the international system in a pluralist way. Overall, the international system has been relying on at least a degree of agreement on basic diplomatic rules, especially in the areas of human rights, democracy, and self-determination, along with the recognition that there is room for disagreement in areas of implementation (Roberts, 2008).[lxxx] Twenty-first century global tensions find their basis in the recognition that different national, cultural, regional, and ideological perspectives lead to many distinct visions of world order (Roberts, 2008).[lxxxi] That is because the current world has a multiplicity of ethical values and a variety of cultural norms that adopt different approaches to international affairs, even though there is a set of established norms. In normative terms, a pluralistic society suggests diversity is healthy because it safeguards individual liberty and promotes debate. Within the realm of international relations, pluralism denotes power is widely and evenly distributed within a society rather than concentrated in the hands of a few.

Hence, the post-Cold War order can be described as an era of group politics that necessitates a high level of international collaboration to understand the many causes of certain global events. This notion also destabilizes the previous western monopoly on international relations theories and how they are employed.

The Rise of China and Non-State Actors in the Post-Cold War Era

Increasing openness to new ideologies and theories, as well as a new and highly interconnected world, have led to the rise of emerging countries, such as China and non-state actors, paving the way for new tensions in the global realm. Principles of democracy and neo-liberal capitalism are at odds with some members of the then-developing world, in particular with China, although the Chinese case is more complex in that it has leveraged the benefits of capitalism and openness for its own benefit while maintaining a firm, authoritarian grip on its internal affairs (Matambo, 2020).[lxxxii] With the rise of emerging countries, the right to spheres of influence is now a legitimate question in international relations theory. As China's rise and America's slow demise seem unstoppable, currently, new theories will be required to sustain a global balance.

However, the rise of non-state actors, like advocacy groups, civil society organizations, multinational corporations, and even terrorist organizations, has added an extra layer of complexity to the study of international relations because they are increasingly wielding more influence over global affairs (Matambo, 2020).[lxxxiii] Until the late 20th century, states were the primary actors governing international relations, and the study of global affairs was predisposed to analyzing the world from the state level. Nevertheless, because it is easier for certain non-state actors to develop within and/or from open societies, they are more likely to pursue the internationalization of democracy while vocally opposing rising authoritarian states (Matambo, 2020).[lxxxiv] In this case, international relations theorization will need to consider ideas promulgated by non-state political activists to maintain its legitimacy.

Lastly, while international organizations were established to ensure peace following World War I and then again after World War II, the post-Cold War era drove them to a greater status of influence. Norms established in the United Nations charter regarding human rights and multilateralism became an intrinsic character of the period after the Cold War. Yet, while the international order was established on those principles, the level to which they were adopted differs among countries. Hence, international organizations have, to some degree, succeeded in maintaining peace and promoting liberal values, but they have also faltered in some cases by being welcoming of entities with different world views. For example, the United Nations has contributed combat troops to peacekeeping missions, negotiated peace settlements that prevented all-out wars, and contained various diseases through World Health Organization initiatives (Sell, 2020).[lxxxv] Nevertheless, the effectiveness of the United Nations has been openly criticized for good reasons. The United Nations Security Council is the most powerful body in terms of capability.

The United States, France, Russia, Great Britain, and China are the only permanent members with the power to veto General Assembly resolutions; thus, they often find themselves at odds with each other. Most of these nations have been the primary movers of global relations for the better part of the 20th century, which raises the prospect of including emerging states to reflect an increasingly pluralist society.

Regional organizations have also emerged to reflect varying spheres of influence, with each one employing different principles to achieve their goals. Contrasting goals have also led to tensions between regions, as well as different potentials for cooperation. Regardless, regional organizations have the power to make common laws for entire groups, which demotes the power state actors held historically. Other international organizations, like the World Bank and International Monetary Fund, have also eroded the nation-state's supremacy.

The rising authority of new actors within the global sphere has shaken and brought into question established international relations theories. On the one hand, international institutions and non-state actors can be deemed ineffective because they fail to prevent conflicts in an anarchic international system. However, the level to which the international system can still be defined as completely anarchic has been brought into question by the rising power of overarching institutions that have had some effect on curtailing belligerent behavior founded in expanding state dominance. The simultaneous and interconnected nature of the current global order requires worldwide cooperation to stifle conflicts, but emerging spheres of influence could and, to some extent, are paving the way for yet another great power competition.

Part II

Theoretical Background

-Realism

-Liberalism

-Constructivism

-Marxism

-Feminism

Zoe's Story

When I chose to study IR, I didn't suspect the intricate journey of jargon the field had in store for me. My professor, Dr. Anne S., loved her jargon, so much so that in the first three classes, I didn't even understand the questions she was asking. She was a big proponent of rationalism - the belief that opinions and theories should be based on reason and knowledge; therefore, talking about scientific realism in her first class sounded like a good idea for her. This description I found at Stanford University's website is eerily close to how she sounded:

> "Scientific realism is a positive epistemic attitude toward the content of our best theories and models, recommending belief in both observable and unobservable aspects of the world described by the sciences. This epistemic attitude has important metaphysical and semantic dimensions, and these various

commitments are contested by a number of rival epistemologies of science, known collectively as forms of scientific antirealism."[lxxxvi]

Now, if you are a well-versed IR professional, the paragraph above is easy to understand. But for a wide-eyed freshman, she might as well have spoken in Zulu. It took some grinding work after classes to simplify the heavily jargon-packed texts to something I could understand and follow. Once I had a solid foundation in the expressions, schools of thoughts, and their significance, it was much easier to keep up with the class.

The following five chapters will present the five dominant schools of thought in international relations, realism, liberalism, constructivism, Marxism, and feminism. Each of these theories evolved over time, attempting to explain the intentions, motivations, and actions of states and later non-state actors. I attempted to make the learning curve about these theories as painless and easy to follow as possible.

While you learn about the five major IR theories, try to be mindful of your reactions – which of them makes the most sense to you, and which of them makes you raise a brow? In other words, try to find which school of thought would represent your way of thinking about the world the best. If you wish, share your discoveries with me either in the form of a review or shoot me an email to zoemckey@gmail.com. *Which IR theory is the closest to your heart/mind? Why?*

Chapter 5: Realism

In academia, realism is a school of thought that focuses on international politics' confrontational, anarchic aspects. Realists consider sovereign states the main actors of IR. States are unitary actors that behave rationally and are led by their individual, national interest. The ultimate goal for them is security and survival. Each state's strength and power dynamic establish their relations with other states.[lxxxvii]

Historical roots

We can find the roots of realism in the ancient writings of Thucydides' *History of the Peloponnesian War*. Remember, we learned extensively about his work in Chapter 1. This war was dated between 431 and 404 B.C.[lxxxviii] In his work, Thucydides searches for the reasons for the Peloponnesian War. He demonstrates how Sparta's negligence of state security and Athens's assertive foreign policy paved the way for authoritarian tendencies in Greece. The Melian Dialogue is an essential part of the war. After invading Melos, Athens proposed to capitulate, but the council of Melos repudiated the demand.[lxxxix] Although emphasizing the relations between the island of Melos and Athens, Thucydides does not consider the specific events to be the cause of the war. He argues the cause of the war was the shift of power balance between the two rival camps. Thus, Athens and Sparta were the leaders of the antagonist sides.[xc]

One may say this dialogue is the first argument between realist and idealist views. The Athenian position was based on realist ideas, as they were talking from the position of power, offering Melos a choice of giving up or annihilation. Melians, on the contrary, wanted justice and suggested neutrality because they thought the gods would back their just cause and their ally, Sparta, would send them military aid. Thus, their worldview is liberal and idealist. In their view, nations have the right to enjoy sovereignty, and war – if unprovoked – is unfair.[xci] We already know how that story went down. Athens said, "Nope, we gave you a chance to resign, and since you didn't, we'll occupy you because... we can."

The Indian scholar Chanakya (370BC-283BC) wrote on the subject of states' power seeking behavior not long after Thucydides. He argued that any king must prioritize the power of the state as the primary goal. In doing so, annihilating the enemies that are trying to undermine this attempt is essential. However, he also advocated for rationality and not sacrificing everything for power. [xcii] Well, if you ask any rational person, it makes a lot of sense.

Despite their early writings, Thucydides and Chanakya were not realists. The concept of realism and IR theory didn't exist in their time – or explicitly any time until the 20th century. However, comparing the rationale and actions of some actors from the ancient world and the modern world, interesting parallels and similarities can be observed. Building upon the repetitive nature of history throughout the centuries, scholars created the theory of realism as an evergreen explanation to human political behavior.

Realism during the Renaissance and the Age of Enlightenment

Why was realism able to survive and thrive for so long? The fundamentals of this theory are based on the intrinsic human desire for security and survival. That is why ancient and modern societies legitimized the use of force by the state, ensuring their safety from others. Although realism is criticized for its skepticism, egoism, insecurity-based views, and drive for power, it would be unimaginable to see a country without law enforcement agencies and courts today.[xciii] The groundwork for today's realist view, the institutions, and a nation-state centered worldview was laid down by a handful of scholars during the European Renaissance (1350s–1650s) and the Age of Enlightenment (early 17th century to early 19th century). The three thinkers I would like to talk about from this period are:

-   Niccolò Machiavelli (1469-1527);

- Thomas Hobbes (1588-1679);
- Jean-Jacques Rousseau (1712-1778).

Niccolò Machiavelli was an Italian philosopher, who challenged the moral traditions of his time. He separated politics from ethics, which was quite unheard of in the Western tradition thus far. His aim is to seek the "effectual truth," not the "imagined" one. Effectual truth consists of, in Machiavelli's view, the sum of the practical conditions that make an individual and the state powerful. Machiavelli is considered a radical realist – he goes as far as ignoring morality as he exclaims "that all means (moral and immoral) are justified to achieve certain political ends." While he acknowledges and approves immoral acts serving a greater good, he also admits they are evil. He stresses that a ruler should be good whenever he can be but should also shy away from using power.[xciv]

In his most prominent work, *The Prince*, Machiavelli emphasizes that a ruler's primary aim should be assuring state security. To perform this important task, the ruler has to embody a lion and a fox at the same time. The lion symbolizes power; the fox is analogous with deception. A good ruler must know when to use either of these affinities to keep its state strong and safe in the international field.

Thomas Hobbes, an English philosopher, in his book *Leviathan*, describes a world where humans are enemies of each other because they are driven by power, distrust, and selfishness. Humans are living in anarchy until a powerful actor, like a state, interferes. Even though the fundamentals of realism come from observing human behavior, the theoretical aspect focuses mainly on states as primary actors in international relations. Realism gives states human-like qualities, like interest, power-seeking, perception of security, and rationalism. In this regard, ancient Sparta and Athens were no exceptions. The struggle for survival is depicted in "The Milian Dialogue," where a very strong Athens destroyed Melos because the latter was not powerful enough to protect itself.[xcv]

The relationship between individuals and the state was the focal point of Thomas Hobbes' philosophy. Although he does not talk much about the relations among countries, his ideas about human relations can be translated to the state level. According to Hobbes, *homo homini lupus est,* meaning man is wolf to man. In other words, it's human nature to behave like a wolf, predatory, cruel, and animalistic, with other humans. Just like humans, states strive to wolf or dominate other nations and territories.[xcvi]

Like a true realist, Hobbes denies the existence of universal moral concepts in global politics. International relations, for him, are no different from human relations. States are egocentric and inimical to each other. However, he does not advocate for violence. Instead, he argues that countries must implement defensive policies to deter other states.[xcvii]

Machiavellianism and Hobbseanism refuse to acknowledge the significance of moral concepts in politics and argue the state must use all methods to realize political goals. Unlike Hobbes, Machiavelli was not against waging war against other states. Critical scholars mention the Machiavellian approach as the biggest flaw of realism. They argue realism is to blame for the confrontational aptitude of modern states, bringing violence and wars into international relations. The doctrine of *raison d'état,* which is a justification for aggressive states' foreign policy aiming to protect national interests, led to the emergence of *Lebensraum*, which Germany used to launch two world wars.[xcviii]

In the article "The State of War," French philosopher Jean-Jacques Rousseau also stresses the states' insecurity and constant strive for power. In other words, the state is a beast that is never satisfied with the amount of power it has. He says, "...it (the state) can always grow bigger; it feels weak so long as there are others stronger than itself. Its safety and preservation demand that it makes itself stronger than its neighbors. It cannot increase, foster, or exercise its strength except at their expense, and even if it has no need to seek for provisions beyond its borders, it searches ceaselessly for new members to give itself a more unshakable position."[xcix]

Not every realist scholar neglects moral issues and ethics in IR. The abovementioned authors were more radical in their views and remained unchallenged by other schools of thought.[c]

Classical Realism

The 20th-century brought about two world wars, global-scale conflicts with casualties never seen before. New explanations were needed in the field of IR to address these new conflicts. This is how (classical) realism was formally born. Authors E.H Carr (1892–1982) and Hans J. Morgenthau (1904–1980) are the founding fathers of classical realism in international relations.

In modern literature, classical realism is often called political realism. Classical realists are skeptical of the moral aspects of international politics but are not oblivious to these notions. Instead, they focus on the realities of the situation and the possible outcomes of policy-based actions. Power is the cornerstone of classical realism but not in the Machiavellian "the end justifies the means" sense. Classical realists don't reject moralism; they are just critical about it. Carr, for instance, condemns idealists for being naïve. In the idealist view, war is an aberration, and living in peace is the normal way of being. People should be educated on how to avoid war and build a peaceful world for everyone. Carr argues that values and morals are subjective, and every state acts according to its best interest. For him, there is only a conflict of interest that can be resolved by power.[ci]

Harmony of interests is an idealist notion based on individuals acknowledging that their goals intersect and can collaborate to resolve their problems. However, Carr offers the concept of conflict of interests and argues life is divided by the interests of people and societies. Furthermore, he thinks countries with a power advantage force weaker states to follow their rules.[cii]

Morgenthau is the first to offer the structural approach to realism and turn it into a complete international relations theory. He wishes to clarify the relationship between interest and morality in IR. Compared to idealists who think international conflicts can be sorted out through negotiation and goodwill, Morgenthau considers power more dominant than morality. In his book, *Politics Among Nations: The Struggle for Power and Peace*, he argues international politics is, in fact, an endeavor for power.[ciii]

He defined six principles that explain classical realism:

1. Realism is governed by objective laws rooted in unchanging human nature.

2. International political leaders act based on their interests defined by power.

3. The concept of interest defined by power is universal, but it can mean many things depending on circumstances.

4. Successful political actions should not be guided by universal moral principles. Prudence, however, should be exercised.

5. States, including one's own, should be judged only as political entities fighting for their personal interests defined by power.

6. Interest defined by power – the cornerstone of politics - can't be subordinated to ethics. However, ethics should be considered, to some extent; otherwise, political actors would be mere beasts. If political actors would only be ethical but not prudent, they would be fools. Balancing power and morality needs to be considered.[civ]

Both Carr's and Morgenthau's work focuses on IR. The way they interpret realism can be used to analyze domestic relations, too. Classical realists see politics as a conflict of interest and power struggle. Peace to them involves accepting and trying to satisfy common interests.

Neo-Realism

Realism has evolved over time. If the first half of the 20th century was dominated by classical realism, it utilized Morgenthau's questionable *Politics Among Nations* textbook as its base. From the 1950s, a new trend popped its head in realism, trying to swap classical realism with a more science-based, reason-driven approach. Realist scholars split into two groups, one being the traditional, non-positivist and the other the scientific – positivist. (Remember my professor's caricaturist description of the latter at the beginning of this chapter?) Later, a third wave of realists emerged, post-positivism.[cv] In practice, traditionalists are prone to ask normative questions and use justifications from history, philosophy, and law. Positivists prefer more rigorous descriptions and explanations, instead of normative answers, when asking questions.[cvi]

Kenneth Waltz was one of the first to formulate new ideas within realism to correct the aspects of classical realism that focused too much on the unprovable assumptions of human nature. Waltz approached realism from a scientific angle, instead of the philosophical nature of Traditional and Classical Realism. According to Waltz, states in the international sphere are like companies in the domestic realm – striving ultimately to survive. Waltz criticizes the previous versions of realism for failing to give proper attention to the international system. They failed to understand and interpret events on the international level. Waltz's neorealism thus can't really be applied to explain domestic issues. The world is not governed by any state but rather by the anarchic nature of the international system – this is the structure. The states are the elements of this system. The absence of international authority forces countries to increase military spending and raise concerns when a neighboring country does so. This is why it is almost impossible to stop a conflict between two reasonably strong states.[cvii]

Waltz distinguishes three key elements of neo-realism:

- The ordering principles of the system.
- The character of the units in the system.
- The distribution of the capabilities of the units in the system.[cviii]

Neo-Realism was also a response to Neo-Liberalism, a school of thought gaining power in academia. The importance of international organizations, like the United Nations, the European Union, and the World Bank, undermined the realist worldview of a state-centered world. Neoliberals, like Robert Keohane and Joseph Nye, criticized realism for its inability to look forward and focus on cooperation rather than a zero-sum game where there is only one winner.[cix]

Offensive and defensive realism

In terms of how the states choose their ultimate goals, scholars distinguish between two types of realism. Kenneth Waltz represents defensive realism, while John Mearsheimer represents offensive realism.

In an anarchic world where countries struggle to stay alive, they need to choose the foreign policy that ensures their security. Waltz argues states are looking for ways to grow their power capacity to outlive all threats. Thus, they concentrate on their security. However, Mearsheimer argues states need to achieve dominance in global politics. He thinks countries should strive to reach hegemony to ensure their safety.[cx]

The Three Assumptions of Realism

1. Statism- the state is the main actor in international relations. The security of the state is its primary goal. In an anarchic world order, states are endlessly competing for power.

2. Survival is the ultimate existential goal for any state. According to Waltz, states seek to increase their power to survive on the political

map. According to Mearsheimer, the state must establish a hegemonic position.

3. Self-help is the third assumption. In a world where there is no higher authority than a state, every state must ensure its security independently.[cxi]

Conclusion

Realism is one of the most influential schools of thought within the realm of International Relations. The history of this theory is vibrant, and it has undergone significant changes over time, from radical realism to neorealism. Although critics have been harsh on the proponents of the realist school, the theory still stands strong as one of the pillars of IR.

Chapter 6: Liberalism

Liberalism has evolved as an advocate for democracy, human rights, free and fair elections, and the rule of law. It is a progressive and idealistic school of thought. Within the realm of international relations, liberalism points out the importance of state sovereignty, institutions, a free-market system, national self-determination, peaceful conflict resolution, and cooperation between state and non-state actors and spreads optimism for the future of humanity.[cxii] States are a part of domestic and international civil societies, and this limits what states can and can't do.

Liberalism portrays the government as an entity that must ensure not only security but also the right of an individual to life, property, and liberty. State oppression is a serious concern for liberal scholars, as they are looking for ways to limit the political and military power of the state. For them, the military expansion of a country is as concerning as domestic oppression. But isn't a militarily strong state a better place to live? No. Liberal authors are against allocating resources to maintain foreign lands under occupation. That is why they came up with the idea of free and fair elections and division of the government into different branches: legislative, executive, and judicial[cxiii].

Historical roots

Unlike realism, the roots of which are traced to Thucydides, liberalism is the product of the seventeenth century's enlightenment movement that "questioned excessive state regulation over individual rights and liberty." This period is characterized by fundamental changes in European societies and transformation from feudalism to capitalism. The zeitgeist of the era groomed a legion of thinkers who spread the ideas of a free market and individual freedom[cxiv].

The center of the work of early liberals was freeing individuals from the two forms of contemporary social constraint—religious conformity and aristocratic privilege. The state and government powers were responsible for perpetuating and enforcing these limitations to individual freedom. The goal of the early liberals was to limit the power of government over individuals and simultaneously hold it accountable to the people.[cxv]

John Locke was the scholar who laid the foundations of liberalism. His idea of a "social contract" is working to this day. Individuals are surrendering some of their rights to the state in exchange for protection of the right to life, freedom, and property. An individual has complete sovereignty over their rights, but the state is the authority that protects those rights. Lock's theory of natural law serves as a basis for liberalism where human rights, private property, and the redistribution of wealth are paramount to ensure everyone's interests, including the poorest.[cxvi]

Jeremy Bentham, another prominent liberal scholar, argued human beings are looking for pleasure and avoiding pain. So the political system should help achieve the greatest amount of happiness or to maximize utility. His theory is called utilitarianism. On the international level, Bentham was an advocate for the creation of international courts to resolve disputes among the states. We can observe the fruits of his ideas today in the International Court of Justice.[cxvii]

Like other major theories, Liberalism was changing through time. Classical liberalism was not the same as liberalism before and after World Wars I and II. In the following sections, we will explore the development of liberalism, not only as a theory but also from a practical point of view.

Classical Liberalism

Peace is the cornerstone of liberalism, and democratic peace theory illustrates this. Democratic peace theorists argue democratic states are generally peaceful because they have checks and balances within the system and perceive other democracies as non-threatening partners.[cxviii] The idealist philosopher, Immanuel Kant, contributed a lot to the idea of peace in international politics. The Kantian doctrine defended individual moral values and was fiercely opposing the Hobbesian "everyone's war against everyone" world. In his pamphlet, "perpetual peace", Kant offered six provisions to ensure peace. These are the following:

- Peace deals should not have options for future wars;
- No state, regardless of its size, shall be acquired, exchanged, gifted, or purchased;

- Abolishment of standing armies;
- National debts shall not be contracted with other states;
- No state is allowed to interfere with the sovereignty of another;
- No state should make agreements at war that could lead to future conflict.[cxix]

Immanuel Kant, Woodrow Wilson, John Stuart Mill, and John Maynard Keynes were the most renowned representatives of classical liberalism. Today, classical liberalism has several distinguished strands:

- republican liberalism argues that using a democratic peace model is the best way to keep international belligerence at bay. Formal representative institutions help connect people to the state. States where institutions most accurately represent the preferences of their people are less likely to end up in international conflict.
- pluralist liberalism argues that social disparities, inequalities, suppression of minorities, and the

violation of individual rights lead to international conflict;

- commercial liberalism believes economic development, cooperation, and interdependence will ensure a more peaceful coexistence;
- regulatory liberalism promotes the formation of international institutions.[cxx]

We should understand that the abovementioned strands of liberalism are stronger together than separately when analyzing foreign policy or conflict. Let's see how liberal values prevented the United States from hopping on the imperialist bandwagon.

In the early 20th century, the United States, while posing as the champion of liberalism, wasn't without imperialistic ambitions. However, on a global scale, the actual size of their colonies was modest at best. Before World War I, the United States controlled a little over 300,000 square kilometers of colonial lands. The German empire claimed around 3 million square kilometers of colonial territory and the United

Kingdom more than 30 million square kilometers.[cxxi]

President Woodrow Wilson believed in liberal values and decided the United States must free Mexico from dictatorship. According to the plot presented by his cabinet, the US forces should capture the cities Veracruz and Tampico and then occupy the east coast of Mexico until the regime changed. Some members of the government were proposing the occupation of Mexico entirely. However, Wilson did not pursue this plan. He stopped the forces at Veracruz and withdrew them in a few months. A negative public opinion in the United States, his personal views, and Mexican hostility have played a significant role in decision-making. [cxxii]

This story of the US with Mexico demonstrates how institutional and normative domestic structures prevented invasion and tempered violence. This kind of behavior can't be seen if liberal norms are not embedded in society. Believing in limiting government power with checks and balances and strong representation and advocating for conquering others is wrong are both liberal notions. Such a society will oppose governmental ambitions that threaten individual liberty. This power dynamic of the early 20th century helped President Woodrow Wilson to stop the US Congress from pursuing an interventionist agenda. The American anti-imperialist zeitgeist, the separation of power, and public opinion prevented American expansion. Growing trade opportunities with Latin American states also halted American imperialism. Just as liberalism predicts, "the absolute gains and opportunities offered by trade, together with preferences for self-determination and non-interference, acted as a restraint on US expansionism toward Mexico in this most imperial of periods in world history."[cxxiii]

Liberalism after World War I

The results of World War I were catastrophic; however, the liberal worldview brought positive light and hope for a better future. But who was the champion of the new peaceful world order? Woodrow Wilson was the biggest practitioner of the liberal school of thought. He outlined fourteen principles that laid a foundation for the creation of a new organization, the League of Nations. Some of Wilson's principles were:

- Open diplomatic relations without shady agreements.
- Free trade to ensure global cooperation.
- The principle of self-determination.

The Association of Nations was later realized in the League of Nations. The Paris Peace conference in 1919 was the platform for the sovereign countries to agree on a new global structure.[cxxiv]

The greatest irony is that the US never became a member of the League of Nations, mostly because of domestic political opposition. The absence of the United States in the League of Nations may have contributed to the failure to keep the global peace. The emergence of radical ideologies of Fascism and Nazism in Italy and Germany put an end to the peaceful coexistence of states. [cxxv]

Liberalism after World War II

The devastating result of World War II denoted hunger for a new world order.

Liberalism was able to dominate over realism yet again.

The principle of self-determination gave practical chances to colonies in Africa and Asia to become sovereign states. Most new countries inherited liberal values, and the citizens in those states began experiencing the benefits of democracy, such as the rights to freedom, free and fair elections, and other social liberties.

Countries that suffered from the war agreed to create viable institutions that would guarantee peaceful coexistence, free trade, security, and dispute resolution through negotiations.

As a result, nationalism was gaining power. However, liberals look at nationalism as a social construct ruled by identifications and organizational structure. Woodrow Wilson saw national self-determination as an inevitable byproduct of democracy.[cxxvi]

Liberal Institutionalism

With the emergence of new states on the world map that realists would see as a possibility for power politics, global institutions, like the United Nations, IMF, EU, and World Bank were also formed.[cxxvii] What was the theory behind the process of creating international organizations? You guessed it right, Liberal Institutionalism. Nation-states wished to create an international political system that would prevent anarchy and self-serving aggression. This theory is regarded as the main criticism of structural realism that propagates anarchy in world politics. Liberal institutionalism envisioned international organizations that transcend rigid national boundaries and create a world in which countries are united by common interests and goals and regulated by principles and rules that serve these interests and goals. The very existence of the United Nations, EU, IMF, and the World Bank proves liberalism is not a utopian theory.[cxxviii]

To illustrate the logic of why the states decided to form international organizations, I would like to mention the functionalist integrations theory. After World War II, Ernst B. Haas offered a theoretical approach to ensure regional integration in Europe. He argued states should become members of the regional organizations, and non-state actors should drive this process. This kind of system would minimize power domination and have a spillover effect on economic, social, and political issues.[cxxix] Can you guess which organization fits this description best? It is the European Union.

Criticism

Criticism is not a strange fruit for liberalism. Throughout history, representatives of different schools of thought were openly arguing against liberal views. Realists and neorealists have been vocal advocates for power politics, thus undermining the core ideas of liberalism. They note that the liberal world was not stable and unable to maintain international order during the World Wars.[cxxx]

As if this criticism was not enough, fellow liberals, who represent a neoliberal school of thought, criticized liberal theory as well. They argue that international organizations are incapable of securing peaceful world order and often bring the example of the US invasion of Iraq in 2003. Neoliberals stressed the failure of the United Nations to support other states that opposed US policy.[cxxxi]

Three assumptions of Liberalism

"Assumption 1. The Nature of Societal Actors.

> Globalization generates differentiated demands from societal individuals and groups with regard to international affairs.

Assumption 2. The Nature of the State.

> States represent the demands of a subset of domestic individuals and social groups, on the basis of whose interests they define "state preferences" and act instrumentally to manage globalization.

Assumption 3. The Nature of the International System.

> The pattern of interdependence among state preferences shapes state behavior."[cxxxii]

Conclusion

Liberalism advocates for democracy, human rights, free and fair elections, and the rule of law. A positive attitude towards the future and mutual benefit is what this theory spreads. For liberal scholars, the state is not naturally aggressive or convergent and is not a primary actor in international relations. They portray individuals and interest groups as the major players in global politics.

Chapter 7: Constructivism

Constructivism is a theory of international relations that has challenged the established understanding of the world. If you are looking for a worldview that is not afraid of going against dogmatic approaches, constructivism is for you. By discussing the intricacies of constructivism, we are entering the post-Cold War era. Constructivism is born because traditional theories, such as liberalism and realism, cannot give a credible answer to the question of why the hostilities between the United States and the USSR have ended so abruptly. There was no major war that brought an end to the bipolar world order, no anarchy, as realism predicted. The bipolar world didn't persist, as neorealism thought. Looking at the world as the state or the international environment as the main driver of dynamic, traditional theories have spent much time observing the agency of individuals. [cxxxiii]

Constructivism argues people are shaping the social world. Influential individuals and ordinary citizens are the main actors in international relations, which by its nature is socially constructed. Let's take Alexander Wendt's illustrative example as proof of the social construction of reality. He said the US feels less threatened by 500 British nuclear weapons than five North Korean ones. It's not the weapons (material structure) that cause the distress but the meaning behind the material structure, the ideational structure – the hostile relationship between the US and North Korea.[cxxxiv]

Scholars of the constructivist school focus on notions like identity and interest. Actors in international relations have a unique identity that shows their interest. The identity of small and large countries differ. Small countries would most likely be preoccupied with assuring their survival, whilst large countries with exercising their power. However, constructivists understand some states might not act according to their identity. This view explains German foreign policy. Despite being the largest economy in Europe, they are not pursuing military expansion. Their World War II history also weighs in this choice.[cxxxv]

To demonstrate that the constructivist approach applies to the real world, let's analyze the example of Bhutan. This small country in the Himalayas is situated between two regional leaders, China and India. Realists would say Bhutan is vulnerable, especially because of the assertive foreign policy of China in Tibet. However, from the constructivist point of view, Bhutan closed its border with China and improved relations with India, thus, showing the small state can have a more flexible foreign policy.[cxxxvi]

Unlike realism and liberalism, which understand the world through power and institutions, constructivism enriched those visions by providing a more resilient understanding of international politics.[cxxxvii] Constructivists emphasize the importance of norms and values in international politics. They argue values, ideas, and beliefs can shape global politics.[cxxxviii] States have certain identities that constitute interests and actions. Once a state pledges to have a certain identity, it is expected to behave in accordance with the norms represented by that identity. We can see this playing out in the case of the many states that have developed climate change mitigation policies. [cxxxix]

Authors identify three types of norms: regulative, constitutive, and prescriptive. The first is responsible for order and constraining behavior, and the second for creating new actors and interests. The third prescribes certain norms.[cxl] The notion of agency and structure plays a central role in constructivism. Agency is the ability of someone to act, whilst the structure is an international system with ideas and beliefs.[cxli]

Historical roots

To talk about the history of constructivism, first, we need to mention the four main reasons constructivism appeared as a theory within the realm of international relations.

- First, many scholars were highly motivated to prove their concepts were right. Therefore, challenging neo-realists and neo-liberalists was a pleasure.[cxlii]

- Second, the end of the Cold War and the emergence of a new world system. We have mentioned that realism and liberalism were unable to predict and explain such events. This was a perfect chance for constructivists to come up with a new vision and challenge existing theories.

- Third, academia was invigorated by the new wave of authors with fresh ideas regarding international relations and the global world order.

- Fourth, constructivists have improved existing ideas offered by old schools of thought.[cxliii]

Constructivism is a modern theory of International Relations. This approach is rooted in the late 1980s, when the world was reshaped. Nicholas Onuf is the founding father of the constructivist theory. He introduced the term in 1989. The primary idea of constructivism is that social interactions are the basis for international relations. Social structures determine the identities and interests of the actors.[cxliv]

However, the history of constructivism started with Immanuel Kant and the nineteenth and twentieth-century Neo-Kantians. According to the Canadian philosopher Ian Hacking, he and Neo-Kantian scholars were the pioneers of constructivism. Kant argued knowledge explains objective reality, and consciousness has to construct reality in our minds. Neo-Kantian scholars took Kant's idea of the knowledge about reality from nature to culture. They have set the human sciences apart from natural sciences. Later, Neo-Kantian scholars Thomas Luckmann and Georg Simmel developed the concept of the social construction of reality. If reality is socially constructed, it is a constructivist idea.[cxlv]

Alexander Wendt contributed heavily to the development of the constructivist theory, demonstrating its viability in international relations. In the article, "Anarchy is What States Make of It", he talks about the fundamentals of constructivism. The article proposes that ideas are more important than the material world because ideas can reshape the world.[cxlvi]

He brings to our attention the concept of reality and knowledge about the world. In academic language, these terms are called ontology and epistemology. Do these words sound hard to understand? They are, in fact, simpler than one may think. The first is about existence, reality, and the material world. The latter is about our knowledge of the world. [cxlvii]

Wendt said countries, like individuals, have perceptions of reality. Based on these notions, different states act diversely on the same issue. Remember the example of how the US perceives the nuclear weapons of England and North Korea differently.[cxlviii]

Constructivism is often presented as if it has had only two scholars, Onuf and Wendt. We will uncover that there are a lot of authors who helped enrich constructivist ideas.[cxlix] Constructivism offers various views on how the world should be. Next, we will explore different theoretical approaches to constructivism.

The debates within constructivism

As an open theory, constructivists criticize not only realists or liberals, but fellow authors as well. The Agent-Structure Debate is one of their most heated arguments to this day. Alexander Wendt criticized Kenneth Waltz's structural theory for the inability to create a new state, constraining only existing ones within the system. The theoretical debate over the issue of whether the state or non-state actors are dominating world politics is also relevant among scholars.[cl] Some authors argue constructivism is not an IR theory at all but rather an ontology or a group of assumptions about the world, agency, and humans.[cli] Do you agree with this argument?

Representatives of German and English schools of thought were the first scholars who contributed to constructivism. Kratochwil, Habermas, and Risse had fierce debates with their English colleagues, Buzan, Hurrell, and others. Apart from these distinguished authors, Scandinavian writers have made their input to constructivism. Walter Carlsnaes, Heikki Patomäki, and Iver Neumann are the prominent names of the Scandinavian constructivist agenda.[clii]

Since constructivism as a theory of international relations is relatively a modern phenomenon, many authors contributed to the creation of different strands of constructivism.

Have you ever heard of strong and weak constructivism? Social scientists of the nineteenth and twentieth centuries, like Wilhelm Dilthey, Edmund Husserl, Max Weber, Thomas Luckmann, and others, were proponents of understanding consciousness in social interactions. These authors made significant input into the development of weak constructivism.

Martin Heidegger, Ludwig Wittgenstein, Peter Winch, and others represent strong constructivism. They argue language is the cornerstone of social interactions and social studies. Unlike them, proponents of weak constructivism argued language is not as important.[cliii]

Modernist linguistic (or 'rules') constructivism

Friedrich Kratochwil and Nicholas Onuf are the most prominent representatives of the modernist linguistic strand of constructivism. They believe that, to understand social reality, we need to uncover the fact that social interactions are constituted by language and rules.[cliv]

Positivists and post-positivists in Constructivism

Positivists pay attention to science as the key to understanding society and international relations. They value empirical methods and experiments when analyzing the world. Post-positivists argued there is a negligible difference between the scientific method and common sense.[clv]

Radical and critical constructivism

The word radical should not scare the reader because it has nothing to do with violence or conflict. Radical constructivists mostly neglect material reality when they analyze a social issue. They rather focus on narratives, discourse, and texts.[clvi]

Constructivism is a critical theory that aims to change society; the existence of critical constructivism should not be a surprise. Critical constructivists take a more pragmatic approach when discussing social problems. Andrew Linklater, Robert Cox, and Antonio Gramsci say, outside human interpretations of the world, material reality exists, nonetheless. Unlike radicals, they prefer to pay attention to material reality as well.[clvii]

Three assumptions of constructivism

This section is dedicated to demonstrating the core assumptions of constructivism that make this theory unique from other schools of international relations and show similarities among them.

First, constructivists have an emphasis on ideas, values, and norms. They cherish the belief that norms, values, and ideas can change the behavior of individuals, thus, the world. They challenge the material structure of international relations proposed by realism and liberalism.[clviii]

Second, the structure of international politics is made by states, the main actors. Alexander Wendt famously stated, "Anarchy is what states are made of." He' agrees that states, as drivers of international relations, are responsible for the nature of IR. For example, the interest the states focus on can determine their behavior – they can choose to behave in an anarchic way, but they can construct a different social reality as well. International relations, therefore, is not anarchic by default. This is contrary to what liberals think.[clix]

Third, international actors shape the structure of international relations, which forces them to be conflictual or cooperative with others. Constructivists see this argument as an opportunity for a change of structure.[clx]

Conclusion

Constructivism emerged at a time when world politics was changing. After the fall of the Berlin Wall, scholars from adjacent disciplines established this unique school of thought. It is a social theory that ascribes significance to ideas, values, and norms that describe and shape the world as we know it. Despite its relative youth, this theory proved itself worthy of standing among realism and liberalism.

The field of international relations is constantly growing. However, it is important to mention what constructivism has added to the discipline. We have already covered different theories of constructivism and can vividly see how much this theory has contributed to the conceptual building block of IR. Theoretical notions, like knowledge, language, social communication, and power, are the contributions worth noting.[clxi]

Chapter 8: Marxism

International relations incorporates various theories that offer their views on the world – so far, we have learned about realism, liberalism, and constructivism. There is one IR theory that is both a critical approach, as it questions the mainstream theories, and a philosophical approach, as it is attached to one of the most renowned German philosophers. That's right, it is Marxism. This theory offers a look into a different reality of the international system in which we live. Even though Marx's ideas are not focused on the establishment of states and their relations, the industrial revolution connects them to IR.[clxii]

Now, before I move on to talk about what Marxism is in international relations, I would like to address a common confusion people have when it comes to Marxism, socialism, and communism. Some folks use these philosophies interchangeably. However, they are not the same thing. Let's explore what's what and what is not:

1. Marxism.

   Both communism and socialism are rooted in Marxism. The latter provides the theoretical framework for the political and economic ideas of socialism and communism. Marxism was born in the late 1800s when Karl Marx and Friedrich Engels formulated a passionate critique against the blossoming capitalism. The industrial revolution exasperated the gap between social classes – the rich got way richer than ever before, while the poor worked in unregulated, inhumane conditions. Anyone who had slavery ancestry - or at the time was still a slave – would have thrown an arm up, thinking, "Yes, we're also working in unregulated, inhuman, and worse, unpaid circumstances!" They would have been right to say so. The difference that triggered some thinkers, like Marx and Engels, into cognitive action was that factories and other industrial establishments were mostly filled with non-slave, white skinned, European people – even children. And their exploitation was unacceptable. Alas came Marxism.

Marx observed that the working class sold their labor as a commodity to the capitalist system that created a surplus for the capitalist owner but not for the laborer. This discrepancy, Marx predicted, would inherently lead to resentment and conflict between the proletariat, or working class, and the bourgeoisie, or the ownership class. As capitalism is grounded in inequality, the working class would eventually revolt against the rich, fundamentally reshaping society, overthrowing capitalism, and establishing a socialist form of government.[clxiii] Marx envisioned this transition happening in stages.

2. Socialism.
The first stage of the Marxian overtaking was socialism. This philosophy envisions public ownership of natural resources and property instead of a private one. The socialist governing style relies on market

cooperation rather than competitiveness. Socialism states that, as every citizen in society contributes to the production of common goods and services, these goods should be shared equally. This is where most capitalists would slam the table and say – *"How is this fair? Why should someone who works hard share the fruits of their hard labor with a work-shy parasite?"* Well, thank you for pointing that out.

Did you know socialist, and later communist, countries in the 1900s had an "anti-parasite" law? In Hungary, for instance, they called people who didn't work "dangerous work avoiders" and got reported to the authorities, and people who weren't employed for a period could face up to one year of jail time and financial penalties for their crime. Every person of an employable age had a booklet to record the date of the start of their employment, the end of it, and the time they spent unemployed. Giving a notice to an employer resulted in retorsion, so people were unlikely to leave a job unless they were fired. The neurotic attempt to have a fully employed society often resulted in people working jobs that were not their specialty or being employed at factories that produced unnecessary goods.[clxiv]

Unlike socialism, capitalism rewards individual effort; one gets their share of the free market based on the amount of work and smarts they put in. The socialist system promised a living wage, free higher education, and free health care in exchange for labor. One can't find the "social scissors" opened as wide in a socialist nation as in a capitalist one that, by default, is doomed to create large discrepancies in inequality – and at its extreme, imperialism.[clxv]

3. Communism.
   Unlike socialism, communism demands not only public ownership of natural resources and property, but also the means of production of goods and

services. For Marx, communism was the proletary utopia, as it didn't divide people because of the competition triggered by a capitalist free market. Marx envisioned communism growing out of socialism in two stages. First, the proletariat would defeat the bourgeoisie and gain control over shaping society. Then, this new society would morph into a classless, governmentless entity, and everybody would live happily, growing into their very best potential.[clxvi]

4. Socialism and Communism Today.
   Today, Marxism-based socialism and communism are still present in various states. China has a communist government; however, it also incorporates some capitalist elements, such as private ownership. They operate in a mixed market economy. Some European countries also have mixed economies where free market meets socialist values, such as free healthcare and higher education. Denmark, Finland, and France are only a few examples. Even the United

States, the citadel of capitalism, has some socialist policies, such as the public school system, free libraries, and Medicaid and Medicare health care support.[clxvii]

Today, there are five countries left that identify as a communist. Can you name them?[2]

I hope the paragraphs above offered a glimpse into the differences between Marxism, socialism, and communism. They are related but not the same thing – they represent a philosophy evolution.

Marxism in IR.

Unlike traditional theories, such as realism or neo-realism, Marxism is against maintaining the status quo in international politics. It wants to change the existing political and social order.[clxviii] Marxists are advocating for contribution to their view of the greater good of humankind. Even

---

[2] Here is the answer: China, Lao, North-Korea, Vietnam, and Cuba. If you though Russia, think again. They technically identify as a "multi-party representative democracy."

though Marxist ideas might seem utopian, they have a deep understanding of social problems and the environment. Marxists argue that modern sovereign states and capitalism are artificial creations of the economic elites and that we should make clear distinctions between capitalist production mode and sovereign countries.[clxix]

The proletariat is the union of the workers around the world. As we previously learned, Marx is concerned about the working conditions and the economic inequality of ordinary workers. One of the main ideas of Marxism is to create a transnational movement of people who suffer under capitalist rule.[clxx] As a critical theory, Marxism seeks not only to show how global capitalism creates class conflicts and economic and political inequalities but to change the system radically with a universal form of emancipation.[clxxi]

Marxism challenges the term "international" in IR. Marxists argue that concepts such as anarchy for realists and international society for the English school[3]

---

[3] The English school, unlike other theories, attempts to give a holistic explanation to why states behave the way they do, looking at the world as a whole. It is built around three concepts: the international system, international society,

mislead humans to believe these concepts are real. According to Marx, the concept of anarchy is an illusion, where states have autonomy, and their acts are predictable as they are "rational actors." But these notions of traditional theories neglect regional inequalities, historical links between the states, and key political and economic actors – such as the proletariat.[clxxii]

---

and world society. The father of the English school, the Australian Hedley Bull, defined these three concepts the following way:

-The international system forms "when two or more states have sufficient contact between them, and have sufficient impact on one another's decisions to cause them to behave as parts of a whole." In other words, the international system incorporates power-seeking states that operate in an anarchic environment.

-The international society forms when states with similar values decide to form and share institutions and follow certain rules when they relate to each other. The goal of an international society is to create and preserve values, rules, and institutions.

-World society transcends international society as "the ultimate units of the great society of all mankind are not states ... but individual human beings." (Stivachtis, Y. (2018, August 6). *Introducing the English School in International Relations Theory*. E-International Relations. Retrieved June 12, 2022, from https://www.e-ir.info/2018/02/23/introducing-the-english-school-in-international-relations-theory/)

Historical roots

There is hardly any theory of international relations that does not have an interesting history. Marxism is no exception. Karl Marx, the father of Marxism, is a nineteenth-century German philosopher and economist, who believed in major changes in the world's modus operandi and materialistic conceptions. Karl Marx was critical of economic liberalism. He thought a liberal economy was not a positive-sum game as its proponents argued. On the contrary, for him, the economy was nothing more than an exploitation of workers by the bourgeoisie – the rich and powerful. The states, according to Marx, were controlled by the ruling elites. [clxxiii]

The first pioneers of Marxist ideas were the communists and revolutionaries of the twentieth century. Vladimir Lenin[4], Rosa Luxembourg[5], and Rudolf Hilferding[6] are

---

[4] Vladimir Lenin, was the founder of the Russian Communist Party (Bolsheviks), inspirer and leader of the Bolshevik Revolution (1917), and the architect, builder, and first head (1917–24) of the Soviet state.
(https://www.britannica.com/biography/Vladimir-Lenin)
[5] Rosa Luxemburg was a Polish-born German revolutionary socialist, Marxist philosopher and anti-war activist.

known for their input in spreading the words of Marx. These scholars and political leaders have created the classical theories of imperialism - how capitalism expanded and led to World War I.[clxxiv]

Vladimir Lenin was one of the most infamous propagandists of the Marxist ideology. He created the Communist Party to take over state power in Russia. Lenin's work, *Imperialism: the Highest Stage of Capitalism,* argued that capitalism has drastically changed. It was exporting capital rather than manufacturing goods. And to protect investments, the states must spend a lot on administrative, economic, military, and naval resources. He identified a two-level structure of the world economy. The first level was the rich center, while the second was the impoverished periphery.[clxxv]

Neo-Marxism

(https://www.britannica.com/biography/Rosa-Luxemburg)
[6] Rudolf Hilferding, Austrian-born German politician who was a leading representative of the Viennese development of Marxism and who served as finance minister in 1923 and 1928 in two German Social Democratic Party (SPD)-led governments.
(https://www.britannica.com/biography/Rudolf-Hilferding)

The term Neo-Marxism is relatively new and has been commonly used since the second half of the twentieth century. The basic approaches, schools of thought, and theories of Neo-Marxism are rooted in classical Marxism. However, there are profound differences between these two theories. For example, rather than focusing only on economic issues, Neo-Marxism was preoccupied with ideology, culture, and the role of capitalist states in a global economy.[clxxvi]

The works of an Italian Marxist scholar, Antonio Gramsci, could be considered pioneering in Neo-Marxism. He tried to find answers to the fundamental questions, such as why the revolutionary movements were so difficult to bring to the western societies, and why the working class refused to rebel against exploitation? He introduces the concept of "hegemony" to deal with these issues.[clxxvii] Hegemony was maintained through the consent of civil society. Domination, an opposing concept to hegemony, was assured through coercion by the state.

Gramsci argued capitalist societies were under constant, hegemonic ideological control. Churches, the media, and the educational system were covering the oppressive and exploitative nature of the capitalist economy. Central and Western European countries were benefiting from both the coercive and consensual means of political and economic power. Unlike classical Marxists, Gramsci was saying the ruling elites needed to get the consent of the exploited class to secure dominance in global politics. For him, political views, ideology, and cultural values were used and spread in society as tools to keep the country under rule.[clxxviii]

The three most prominent theories at the heart of the Neo-Marxist school of thought are the world-system theory, dependency theory, and critical international relations theory.

World System Theory

Marxist scholars have been contributing to the development of critical literature about the unfairness of the capitalist world. In the 1970s, the World System Theory appeared as a critique of capitalism and how it affects a post-colonial world. This theory, inspired by Lenin's fundamental work, *Imperialism - The Highest Stage of Capitalism*, identifies a two-level structure within the capitalist model of the global economy. The dominant structure is called the core or center, which represents developed countries. The less-developed structure is called the periphery. Periphery, as you correctly guessed, represents the less developed states.[clxxix]

Immanuel Wallerstein, an American sociologist, contributed to the development of this World System Theory. In 1974, he analyzed the realities of the late twentieth century and offered a long-term vision of the history of states.[clxxx] In *Modern World System: Capitalist Agriculture and the Origins of the European World Economy in the Sixteenth Century*, he discusses the evolution of capitalism to sixteenth-century Europe. Wallerstein identifies three levels within the capitalist system: the core/center, periphery, and semi-periphery were distinguished by the amount of accumulated wealth and economic development. According to Wallerstein, peripheral regions during post-colonial times were impoverished and served as the providers of raw materials to the core. Core countries had strong banking systems, advanced agriculture, and manufacturing. The issue with capitalism in the eyes of Wallerstein was that the core exploited cheap labor from the periphery and got richer, while the periphery did not enjoy development and stayed poor.[clxxxi]

Wallerstein's world system theory also mentions semi-periphery, which was in-between the core and periphery in terms of production and wealth. The semi-periphery, unlike peripheral states, was somewhat wealthier but not nearly as rich as the core that imported labor from the semi-periphery, as well. Examples of semi-peripheral countries would be Taiwan and Singapore. They, unlike Bhutan, a periphery state, are more prosperous and have modern means of production but still can't be considered as powerful as the United States or Germany.[clxxxii]

Dependency Theory

Marxist scholars have written a lot about inequalities between developed and undeveloped parts of the world. The second Neo-Marxist branch is the Dependency Theory.

Andre Gunder Frank[7], Fernando Henrique Cardoso[8], and Enzo Faletto[9] are the most renowned authors on this subject. Their work focused on Latin America because they wanted to explain why this region was growing and

---

[7] German-American sociologist and economic historian.
[8] Brazilian sociologist and teacher.
[9] Chilean sociologist.

stagnating despite its richness in natural resources.

The abovementioned authors identified two reasons Latin America was struggling. The first is an internal reason; the second is external. Internal reasons include issues like inter-class relationships in the country, historical realities of the state, and the existing -often corrupt and abusive - political system. External problems are the dominant position of foreign capital, multinational corporations that were buying domestic resources, and the global political and economic regime under capitalism. According to the proponents of dependency theory, Latin American countries can't sustain themselves internally in the long run.[clxxxiii]

Critical International Relations Theory

The last two decades of the twentieth century brought significant changes to international politics. Marxism has gone through a transformation. If you remember, we touched on critical IR theory in constructivism. We also mentioned some of these distinguished authors, Robert W. Cox[10], Richard Ashley[11], Andrew Linklater[12], and Mark Hoffman.[13] [clxxxiv]

What is the difference between these scholars and earlier Marxists? They are concerned with philosophical questions of ontology, epistemology, and normativity in international relations. But what drove these authors to develop critical theory? Emancipation is the main reason for the emergence of critical IR theory. Their goal is to transform international relations and abolish obstacles toward equality and universal freedom. Also, the critical international theory is against positivist and rationalist theories of international relations, such as realism, neo-realism, liberalism, or neo-liberalism. Cosmopolitanism, universal justice, and equality are the terms often used by critical theorists, who see social structures as intersubjective and socially constructed. They critique dogmatism, power-relations, and status-quo, often the pillars of traditional theories, such as realism. In a way, critical IR theory is a means to question and delegitimize the current status of power and privilege. The ultimate goal of this theory is to establish an alternative

---

[10] Canadian political science scholar and former United Nations officer.

[11] American international relations scholar.

[12] British international relations academic.

[13] American international relations expert.

approach to international relations and replace hierarchical power relations with emancipation. [clxxxv]

Borders, Migration, and Marxism

When we are talking about emancipation, cosmopolitanism, and universal freedom, it is impossible to avoid the subject of migrations and border issues in international relations.

Marxists dislike borders in international relations, as they are creating impediments to access to goods, resources, and labor. Some scholars even argue that modern international relations should have no political borders at all and that the concept of global citizenship will ensure benefits for everyone. In their opinion, capitalism unites all oppressed people, and because of the system, their needs are neglected. [clxxxvi]

Marxists are critical of migration policies conducted by the European states. First, even though there is a 1951 Refugee Convention, the states still need to give consent to the treaty, which does not guarantee the possibility of migration, even though the convention does. Second, economic migrants are in an even worse position. European states make political decisions on who is a "good" migrant; otherwise, they are just closing borders to everyone else. They legitimize and take in people with skills and knowledge. Although the migration of people predated capitalism, the process of privatization led to people fleeing their homeland. The wealthy landowners were fencing their lands, which prevented ordinary people from using the land as before. Also, wealthy citizens were buying out the adjacent lands from impoverished farmers who could not compete with industrial capabilities. According to Marxist scholars, this forced people to sell their land and labor to capitalist elites.[clxxxvii]

Three Assumptions of Marxism

The three core assumptions of Marxism are:

Assumption 1:
Economic and materialistic determinism is the cornerstone of the Marxist ideology. Marxism considers economic inequalities as the most important problem in any state or global politics. In other words, the economy is the base,

while politics, religion, culture, and education are superstructures that depend on the economy.

Assumption 2:

The concept of class and struggle is central in international relations. In every society, the economic elite or bourgeoisie controls the state and exploits the labor of ordinary workers. Conflicts emerge because of class differences.

Assumption 3:

The proletariat or workers' revolution is the only way to establish peace. The goal of the revolution is to establish a classless society worldwide.[clxxxviii]

Conclusion

Marxism offers a profoundly different view on international relations. Unlike classical theories, such as realism or liberalism, Marxism wants to get rid of the existing status quo and bring radical social and political transformation. Marxist and Neo-Marxist scholars are critical of the capitalist political order, which, in their view, creates injustices and exploitation of the labor of undeveloped states. They propose a classless world and cosmopolitan views, where a proletariat revolution is a tool to emancipation.

Chapter 9: Feminism

So far, we have covered traditional theories of international relations, such as realism and liberalism, and talked about critical theories, like constructivism and Marxism. In this chapter, we're going to learn about one of the most recent theories, feminism. International relations is constantly trying to be on foot with modern global politics and understand how the world operates, and feminism contributes with a thus far unexplored angle - how women have been absent and marginalized in politics and decision-making throughout the centuries. IR has constantly been under criticism for being gender blind. Feminist scholars have challenged these basic concepts and assumptions of international relations, deconstructing gender, both as a socially constructed identity and an organizing idea. This meant first acknowledging and then challenging the roles men and women hold in global politics. Thanks to feminism, these roles are slowly changing, as public attention has been turned to the inequalities women have in representation, payment, and possibilities.

The journey involved uncovering the issue of gendered violence. Making violence against women visible in global politics was essential and was a successful hit against existing assumptions of the international system that neglected the impact these events had on the everyday life of women. Former UN Secretary-General, Ban Ki-Moon, has launched a campaign to end violence against women. This is a global issue, and over 600 million women live in regions and countries where domestic violence is rampant, and its impact is neglected. Some of these countries present themselves as safe, peaceful, and democratic. In general, women do not have as many political, economic, and social rights and power as men do. The feminist approach challenges an established perception of the security agenda that is proposed by traditional theories and schools of thought in IR. Feminism argues the exclusive nature of gender politics is obvious. For example, even though women are more likely to populate the areas where security is an issue and conflicts are rampant, gendered exclusion is highly present. Feminist scholars, therefore, are demonstrating the need for inclusive politics that emphasizes and allows the contribution of women in politics.[clxxxix]

One of the central goals of feminism is to transform international politics to be more inclusive. Institutions and decision-making positions are not represented equally; they are dominated by men. For instance, the national parliaments worldwide were represented by women in only 22.9% of cases, according to the World Bank's statistics of 2015. [cxc] According to some major 2022 studies, despite women representing 54.3% of the US workforce, only 35% are in senior leadership positions, and only 8.2% are Fortune 500 CEOs. The numbers are improving compared to past decades, but women are still underrepresented in world-leading positions. These numbers look direr if we check the statistics of less developed countries or the situation of women of color.[cxci]

We need to distinguish between sex and gender. The former is about human physiology, while the latter is a social construct. The feminine side of any issue is perceived as less relevant, irrational, or something that needs protection. These types of social constructs make it extremely challenging for women to access the streams of power and thus influence global politics. Over time, feminism has fought for women's rights, gender equality, women's right to vote, work, earn equal pay, hold public office, own property, get educated, be an equal partner in marriage, have maternity leave, ensure contraception, legal abortion, social integration, protection from sexual harassment, and domestic violence. Some of these things are normal in Western societies, which proves the success of the movement. However, women didn't enjoy many -or any- of these freedoms decades ago. Let's see how feminism started and evolved over the centuries. [cxcii]

Historical Roots

The eighteenth-century English writer, Mary Wollstonecraft, is considered to be the founder of feminism. Her main focus is women's rights to education. She argues women are not naturally inferior to men, but the lack of education prevents them from being on the same level of success. Another pioneer of the feminist ideology was Olympe De Gouges of France. She advocated for women's rights during and after the French Revolution in the late eighteenth century. Frederick Engels' work in the late nineteenth century also touches on the issue of women's oppression, which was the fault of the introduction of private property. The capitalist model of economy and industrialization separates social classes into private and public domains. As a result, women are predominantly excluded from the public domain because it is exclusively comprised of male workers.[cxciii]

Historically, there have been four waves of the feminist movement. The first happened between the 19th to early-20th centuries, the women's suffrage movement, mainly fighting for women's voting rights. In the 1960s, the second wave campaigned for legal and social equality for women. In the early 1990s, the third wave of feminism focused on the respect of individuality and diversity. The fourth wave is still happening, but it started around 2012. The most well-known aspect of this wave is the Me Too movement that uses social media to fight workplace and other types of sexual harassment and violence against women.[cxciv]

Concerning the discipline of international relations, feminism gained a more powerful global significance in the 1960s and 1970s. In the 1980s, the field of IR was largely male-dominated, thus, feminism was criticized by scholars. Also, the central issues of IR were war and international diplomacy. *Millenium,* the first journal in the field of IR that dedicated special attention to the feminist movement, argued international relations were excessively covering the issues of war, anarchy, statecraft, and fear but neglected other critical problems, such as the realities of women. Contributors of *Millenium,* Ann Tickner, Spike Peterson, Jan Jindy Pettman, and others, argued power politics and the state-centric approach of IR fails to provide a holistic picture of the world as it is. Some authors contested bias toward women's perception and argued women understood international relations better because they were not part of biased institutions. For instance, Tickner stated IR concepts were exclusively derived from male experiences. She argued Hans Morgenthau's six principles of power are a vivid example of a masculine perception.[cxcv]

Feminism in IR has many theories that have been in close contact with liberalism, constructivism, and Marxism. So next, we will explore these theories and understand how they interpret the world.

Liberal Feminism

Liberal feminism started developing in the eighteenth-century phenomenon. I mentioned the early champions, Olympe de Gouges from France and Mary Wollstonecraft from Britain. Their concern was that women needed to be empowered to create a society of equal opportunities and possibilities. They saw women as human beings and as rational actors whose role was to fulfill their interests and protect their innate rights. The biggest issue that liberal feminists have identified is that women were tied down to domestic problems without an opportunity to develop other social skills. They believed men and women are equal, and it was essential to ensure women's presence in high political places. Reformist rather than a revolutionary approach was liberal feminists' way of changing gender imbalance. Among liberal feminists was the French Philosopher Simone de Beauvoir.[cxcvi]

Contrary to liberal feminists, Marxists saw revolution as a solution to the oppression of women as a social class. They criticized liberal feminists for their idea that men were the oppressors of women. Instead, they argued that capitalism and social class differences were to blame for gender injustices. *The origins of the Family, Private Property, and the State,* written by Frederick Engels in 1884, served as a foundation for Marxist feminism. Marxists thought there was no room for women's rights and equality in class society. Women were providing an additional labor force to capitalist elites. Thus, they were an exploited class. To break this cycle, Marxists advocated for women's participation in the wider struggle against the capitalist model.[cxcvii]

Socialist feminists were highly critical of gender inequality. Unlike Marxists, they argued the oppression of women predated capitalist societies. Socialists identified another central reason for the unequal treatment of women - the patriarchal system and male dominance.[cxcviii]

Radical Feminism

Radical feminism is very critical of the Marxist and Socialist approaches. Marxist and socialist feminism define capitalism as the main barrier that prevents equality between men and women. Radical feminist authors, however, claim patriarchy is the main problem in social and global relations. They want to develop a women-centered approach in academia that challenges male-oriented values and structures. Liberal feminism is an insufficient interpretation and representation of feminism in the radicals' eyes.[cxcix]

Postmodernist Feminism

Cultural biases, marginality, and unequal treatment have brought us to where we are today. Postmodern feminism seeks to uncover the universal truth in a world of biases and assumptions. Scholars of this school of thought describe gender not in terms of identity or social structure but in terms of discourse. Inequalities cannot be understood as a natural phenomenon but rather a discourse about the human body being objectified, sexual differences, and inequalities being neglected. Charlotte Hooper, postmodern feminist scholar, stated one can't fully understand international relations unless one also understands the implications of the fact that it is led mainly by men. Therefore, postmodern feminism calls for more women authors to help understand discourse and change it.[cc]

Christine Sylvester, a postmodern feminist, popularized the method of world-traveling. This means, "traveling to difference and recognizing it." Feminism has received criticism for spreading mainly Western values, almost forcing women from different cultures to assimilate and yield to these conceptualizations. Sylvester's method "is intended to address exclusions within feminist IR, especially Third World feminist criticisms of the dominance of the white, Western female subject in the conceptual framing of feminist analyses of gender and international development and women's human rights, for example."[cci]

Critical Theory

Gramscian Marxism influenced the creation of the critical theory of feminism. For feminist critical theorists, identifying a discourse is not enough. They are looking for ways to connect theories with social practices. Therefore, social institutions need to be transformed. Critical feminists argue theories always have an addressee and purpose. They came up with two ways of transforming social institutions. The first is agonistic, which is a model to understand how to define social agents. The second is normative, to define what justice is in a new social reality.[ccii]

Feminist Constructivism

The constructivist view gives the basis for feminist constructivism. By the way, do you remember what constructivism says? Constructivism argues that, in international relations, reality is a social construct, and these ideas, norms, and values shape our world. Feminist constructivism takes a different approach. It argues that the idea of how gender influences world politics is paramount. They note the gender differences between women and men are unlike anatomical differences; they are social and cultural constructs. Elisabeth Prugl, in her book, *The Global Construction of Gender,* mentioned that gender politics led to the creation of a system where women are home-based workers. Therefore, inadequate working conditions and low wages are justified on the premise that home-based work is not essential.[cciii]

Post-Colonial Feminism

The western model of world politics has influenced former colonies, and to this day, the norms, values, and perceptions are predominantly western. Post-colonial feminism focuses on gender roles in a social, political, and economic environment that doesn't necessarily adhere to and agree with the western model. These scholars argue that international organizations need to consider local social and cultural norms instead of evaluating postcolonial countries from a western perspective.

Chandra Mohanty, in her essay, "Under Western Eyes: Feminist Scholarship and Colonial Discourses", argued that the role of women in society should be analyzed within their cultural context. In her opinion, universal standards are not offering a viable solution for a specific cultural set of norms. Therefore, race, class, and regional geography must be taken into consideration.[cciv]

Feminism and Peacekeeping

One of the central concerns of IR is security and maintaining peace as conflicts are getting more complex. Peacekeeping missions are standard when it comes to conflict resolution. Throughout history, the United Nations has conducted many such missions. Feminists, however, argue that peacekeeping is conducted from a masculine point of view. The post-conflict period is also characterized by violence against women. From 1993 to 2014, the number of women in peacekeeping missions was not enough. A study conducted by Radhika Coomaraswamy in 2015 reiterates the grave situation with under-resourced gender issues in peacekeeping.[ccv]

Three assumptions of feminism

Let us discuss the core assumptions of feminism in International Relations. The three main points of argument within the feminist approach are:

First assumption:

Feminism advocates for women's rights and explains why there is a disadvantage between men and women.

Second assumption:

The social structures and practices are male dominated. Therefore, the subordination of women is because of the patriarchal nature of the system.

Third assumption:

Because of the abovementioned premises, feminists have contributed their views and solutions to the theoretical approach to international relations.[ccvi]

Conclusion

Feminism gained power relatively recently in international relations. However, the history of the feminist ideology goes back to the French Revolution. As we have seen, the main goal of feminism is to challenge the exclusive, male-dominant nature of international politics and offer a different, inclusive, and holistic approach to problems. The academic struggle to be acknowledged has resulted in the emergence of different theories within feminism that now are part of mainstream politics.

Final Words

Our delving into the historical and theoretical background of international relations ends here, but our journey into the field has just started. By reading this book, you gained some insight into how policy makers understand the world and what theories they might use to base their perceptions of state behavior. They often devise solutions to national and international problems using the IR theories you read about. These solutions can turn into strategic policies that aim to fulfill national goals. In the mind of a realist leader, these policies may be targeted to increase the state's influence and power relative to other states. A liberalist leader, on the other hand, may institute policies that target the increase of international trade and interdependence. A constructivist policy maker would create international law and norm-heavy action plans.

This book aimed to show which theories influence decision-makers the most, what world views these people can have, and how their policy-development impacts the state, the international sphere, and the life of everyday citizens like you and me.

Respectfully,

Albert Rutherford and Zoe McKey

References

Ankit Tomar. (n.d.). Theories of International Relations and World History. Http://Dcac.Du.Ac.In/. Retrieved April 16, 2022, from http://dcac.du.ac.in/documents/E-Resource/2020/Metrial/410MukeshBagoria1.pdf

Ariella, S. (2022, April 21). *25 Women In Leadership Statistics [2022]: Facts On The Gender Gap In Corporate And Political Leadership – Zippia.* Zippier. Retrieved June 4, 2022, from https://www.zippia.com/advice/women-in-leadership-statistics/

Binu Joseph. (n.d.). Liberalism: A Brief Understanding of Liberal Theory in International Relations. Https://Www.Academia.Edu/. Retrieved April 16, 2022, from https://www.academia.edu/37173609/LIBERALISM_A_Brief_Understanding_of_Liberal_Theory_in_International_Relations

Biswas, A. (n.d.). Realism Theory In International Relations In Detail. School of Political Science. Retrieved May 18, 2020, from https://schoolofpoliticalscience.com/realism-theory-in-international-relations/

Bjork, P. (2021, March 4). *A Brief Look at the Four Waves of Feminism.* TheHumanist.Com. Retrieved June 5, 2022, from https://thehumanist.com/commentary/a-brief-look-at-the-four-waves-of-feminism/

Cameron, F. (2014, July 8). The Impact of the First World War and Its Implications for Europe

Today | Heinrich Böll Stiftung. Heinrich-Böll-Stiftung. Retrieved April 5, 2022, from https://www.boell.de/en/2014/07/08/impact-first-world-war-and-its-implications-europe-

today#Who%20caused%20the%20War?

Camisão, S. A. A. I. (2018, August 6). Introducing Realism in International Relations Theory. E-International Relations. Retrieved May 18, 2022, from https://www.e-ir.info/2018/02/27/introducing-realism-in-international-relations-theory/

Campbell, S. L. (2018, June 26). *The Differences Between Marxism, Socialism & Communism*. Classroom.Synonym. Retrieved June 4, 2022, from https://classroom.synonym.com/difference

s-between-marxism-socialism-communism-17064.html

Chakravartty, A. (2017, June 12). *Scientific Realism (Stanford Encyclopedia of Philosophy)*. Stanford Encyclopedia of Philosophy. Retrieved June 1, 2022, from https://plato.stanford.edu/entries/scientific-realism/

Constructivism in International Relations. (n.d.). International Affairs Forum. Retrieved April 16, 2022, from https://www.ia-forum.org/Content/ViewInternal_Document.cfm?contenttype_id=5&ContentID=8773

Emanuel Adler. (2002). Constructivism and International Relations. Https://Omnilogos.Com/. Retrieved April 16, 2022, from https://omnilogos.com/constructivism-and-international-relations/

Faqi Ahmad. (2020, October 11). The Theory of Constructivism in International Relations. Https://Www.Academia.Edu/. Retrieved April 16, 2022, from https://www.academia.edu/44540969/The_Theory_of_Constructivism_in_International_Relations

Hindley, M. (2017). World War I Changed America and Transformed Its Role in International Relat. The National Endowment for the Humanities. Retrieved April 5, 2022, from https://www.neh.gov/humanities/2017/summer/feature/world-war-i-changed-america-and-transformed-its-role-in-international-relations

Jacqui True. (2017, February 30). Feminism and Gender Studies in International Relations Theory. Oxford Research Encyclopedia of International Studies. Retrieved April 16, 2022, from https://oxfordre.com/internationalstudies/view/10.1093/acrefore/9780190846626.001.0001/acrefore-9780190846626-e-46

Jeffrey W. Meiser. (2018, February 18). Introducing Liberalism in International Relations Theory. E-International Relations. Retrieved April 16, 2022, from https://www.e-ir.info/2018/02/18/introducing-liberalism-in-international-relations-theory/

Larcinese, V. (2007, January 11). *Does Political Knowledge Increase Turnout? Evidence from the 1997 British General Election on JSTOR*. Public Choice, Vol. 131, No. 3/4,

2007, Pp. 387–411. JSTOR. Retrieved May 31, 2022, from https://www.jstor.org/stable/27698109

Lerner, M. (n.d.). *liberalism - Classical liberalism.* Encyclopedia Britannica. Retrieved June 1, 2022, from https://www.britannica.com/topic/liberalism/Classical-liberalism

Lianboi Vaiphei. (n.d.). Feminist Perspectives and International Relations. Http://Dcac.Du.Ac.In/. Retrieved April 16, 2022, from http://dcac.du.ac.in/documents/E-Resource/2020/Metrial/409MukeshBagoria2.pdf

Lobell, S. E. (2010, March 1). *Structural Realism/Offensive and Defensive Realism.* Oxford University Press. Retrieved June 1, 2022, from

https://oxfordre.com/internationalstudies/vi
ew/10.1093/acrefore/9780190846626.001.
0001/acrefore-9780190846626-e-304

Matambo, E. (2020, April 22). International
Relations Theory after the Cold War:
China, the Global South and Non-state
Actors. E-International Relations.
Retrieved April 14, 2022, from
https://www.e-
ir.info/2020/04/21/international-relations-
theory-after-the-cold-war-china-the-global-
south-and-non-state-actors/

Maïa Pal. (2018, February 25). Introducing
Marxism in International Relations
Theory. E-International Relations.
Retrieved April 16, 2022, from
https://www.e-
ir.info/2018/02/25/introducing-marxism-
in-international-relations-theory/

Mock, G. (2018, November 8). How the Trauma and Struggles of World War I Helped Shape the

Modern. Duke Today. Retrieved April 5, 2022, from https://today.duke.edu/2018/11/how-trauma-and-struggles-world-war-i-helped-shape-modern-world

Moravcsik, A. (n.d.). Liberalism and International Relations Theory. Princeton.Edu. Retrieved April 16, 2022, from https://www.princeton.edu/~amoravcs/library/liberalism_working.pdf

Moravcsik, A. (2011, July). *The New Liberalism.* The Oxford Handbook of Political Science. Retrieved June 3, 2022, from https://www.oxfordhandbooks.com/view/10.1093/oxfordhb/9780199604456.001.0001/oxfordhb-9780199604456-e-033

Naranjo, R. (2018, January 18). Historical analysis of the Cold War. eHistory. Retrieved April 14, 2022, from https://ehistory.osu.edu/articles/historical-analysis-cold-war

Pfaltzgraff Jr., R. (2019). World War I and IR Theory. The Fletcher Forum of World Affairs, 43(1).
https://www.jstor.org/stable/45289824

Political Realism in International Relations (Stanford Encyclopedia of Philosophy). (2017, May
24). Stanford Encyclopedia of Philosophy. Retrieved May 18, 2022, from https://plato.stanford.edu/entries/realism-intl-relations/

Roberts, A (2008). International Relations after the Cold War. International Affairs (Royal Institute of International Affairs 1944-),

84(2)   ,   335-350.
http://www.jstor.org/stable/25144768

Sarah Smith. (2018, January 4). Introducing
Feminism in International Relations
Theory. E-International Relations.
Retrieved April 16, 2022, from
https://www.e-
ir.info/2018/01/04/feminism-in-
international-relations-theory/

Sell, T. (Ed.). (2020). Post-Cold War International
Relations. In A Primer on Politics.
https://socialsci.libretexts.org/.

Sarina Theys. (2018, April 23). Introducing
Constructivism in International Relations
Theory. E-International Relations.
Retrieved April 16, 2022, from
https://www.e-
ir.info/2018/02/23/introducing-

constructivism-in-international-relations-
theory/

Snyder III, R. E. (2011, December). *The impact of age, education, political knowledge and political context on voter turnout.* University of Nevada. Retrieved May 31, 2022, from https://digitalscholarship.unlv.edu/cgi/view content.cgi?article=2401&context=thesesd issertations

The Cold War and its impact on international relations. (2021, May 27). iPleaders. Retrieved April 14, 2022, from https://blog.ipleaders.in/cold-war-impact-international-relations/

The Cold War: International Relations between 1945 and 1989 | Free Essay Example. (2020, September 4). StudyCorgi.Com. Retrieved April 14, 2022, from https://studycorgi.com/the-cold-war-international-relations-between-1945-and-1989/#:%7E:text=The%20Cold%20War%20significantly%20influenced%20the%20nature%20and,interest%20and%20the%20competition%20for%20nuclear%20supremacy.%20

To-retro Blog. (2018, September 30). *Közveszélyes munkakerülés - ma már nevetségesnek tűnik, régen simán börtön járt érte | szmo.hu*. Szeretlek Magyarország. Retrieved June 4, 2022, from https://www.szeretlekmagyarorszag.hu/multunk/kozveszelyes-munkakerules-ma-mar-nevetsegesnek-tunik-regen-siman-borton-jart-erte/

Wisidagama, S. (2017, July 7). The Evolution of International Relations as a Field of Activity to

International Relations as an Academic Discipline. Academia. Retrieved April 7, 2022, From https://www.academia.edu/33799619/The_ Evolution_of_International_Relations_as_ a_F

ield_of_Activity_to_International_Relation s_as_an_Academic_Discipline

Why is International Relations a discipline? (2019, August 7). Nottingham Trent University Online. Retrieved April 7, 2022, from https://online.ntu.ac.uk/online-student-experience/articles/international-relations-discipline-it-important

Yilmaz, M. (2008). "The New World Order": An Outline of the Post-Cold War Era. Turkish Journal of International Relations, 7(4).

Endnotes

[i] Snyder III, R. E. (2011, December). *The impact of age, education, political knowledge and political context on voter turnout*. University of Nevada. Retrieved May 31, 2022, from https://digitalscholarship.unlv.edu/cgi/viewcontent.cgi?article=2401&context=thesesdissertations

[ii] Larcinese, V. (2007, January 11). *Does Political Knowledge Increase Turnout? Evidence from the 1997 British General Election on JSTOR*. Public Choice, Vol. 131, No. 3/4, 2007, Pp. 387–411. JSTOR. Retrieved May 31, 2022, from https://www.jstor.org/stable/27698109

[iii] Chairil, T. (2013, September 26). Historic Antecedents of Realist IR Theories (1): Thucydides.

International Relations BINUS University. https://ir.binus.ac.id/2013/09/26/historic-

antecedents-of-realist-ir-theories-1-thucydides/

[iv] Chairil, T. (2013, September 26). Historic

Antecedents of Realist IR Theories (1): Thucydides.

International Relations BINUS University.
https://ir.binus.ac.id/2013/09/26/historic-

antecedents-of-realist-ir-theories-1-thucydides/

[v] Morley, N. (2020). Thucydides and International
Relations. Omnibus.

[vi] Chairil, T. (2013, September 26). Historic
Antecedents of Realist IR Theories (1): Thucydides.

International Relations BINUS University.
https://ir.binus.ac.id/2013/09/26/historic-

antecedents-of-realist-ir-theories-1-thucydides/

[vii] Chairil, T. (2013, September 26). Historic
Antecedents of Realist IR Theories (1): Thucydides.

International Relations BINUS University.
https://ir.binus.ac.id/2013/09/26/historic-

antecedents-of-realist-ir-theories-1-thucydides/

[viii] Chairil, T. (2013, September 26). Historic
Antecedents of Realist IR Theories (1): Thucydides.

International Relations BINUS University.
https://ir.binus.ac.id/2013/09/26/historic-

antecedents-of-realist-ir-theories-1-thucydides/

[ix] Chairil, T. (2013, September 26). Historic Antecedents of Realist IR Theories (1): Thucydides.

International Relations BINUS University. https://ir.binus.ac.id/2013/09/26/historic-

antecedents-of-realist-ir-theories-1-thucydides/

[x] Morley, N. (2020). Thucydides and International Relations. Omnibus.

[xi] Morley, N. (2020). Thucydides and International Relations. Omnibus.

[xii] Debnar, P. (2017). Thucydides' Melian Dialogue: Commentary, Text, and Vocabulary (1st ed.).

Paula Debnar.

[xiii] Biggs, J. (2018, June 2). Thucydides the

Neorealist? Https://Bookdown.Org/Jack_Biggs/Thucydides_Disser tation/. Retrieved

March 29, 2022, from

https://bookdown.org/Jack_Biggs/Thucydides_Disserta tion/chapter-1-neorealism-

and-thucydides.html

[xiv] Morley, N. (2020). Thucydides and International Relations. Omnibus.

[xv] Morley, N. (2020). Thucydides and International Relations. Omnibus.

[xvi] CBS News. (2022, March 31). Russia says it's building a new "democratic world order" with

China. CBS News. Retrieved March 29, 2022, from

https://www.cbsnews.com/news/russia-china-lavrov-visit-beijing-vladimir-putin-xi-

jinping-new-world-order/

[xvii] Morley, N. (2020). Thucydides and International Relations. Omnibus.

[xviii] Morley, N. (2020). Thucydides and International Relations. Omnibus.

[xix] Morley, N. (2020). Thucydides and International Relations. Omnibus.

[xx] Bagby, L. M. J. (1994). The use and abuse of Thucydides in international relations. International

Organization, 48(1), 131–153. https://doi.org/10.1017/s0020818300000849

[xxi] Bagby, L. M. J. (1994). The use and abuse of Thucydides in international relations. International Organization, 48(1), 131–153. https://doi.org/10.1017/s0020818300000849

[xxii] Bagby, L. M. J. (1994). The use and abuse of

Thucydides in international relations. International

Organization, 48(1), 131–153.
https://doi.org/10.1017/s0020818300000849

[xxiii] Bagby, L. M. J. (1994). The use and abuse of
Thucydides in international relations. International
Organization, 48(1), 131–153.
https://doi.org/10.1017/s0020818300000849

[xxiv] Bagby, L. M. J. (1994). The use and abuse of
Thucydides in international relations. International

Organization, 48(1), 131–153.
https://doi.org/10.1017/s0020818300000849

[xxv] Mason, E. (2020, May 23). The 1618 Defenestration
of Prague explained. History Extra.

Retrieved March 22, 2022, from
https://www.historyextra.com/period/stuart/1618-

defenestration-

prague-facts-history-explained-what-
happened-why-castle-protestant-catholic/

[xxvi] International Relations. (2013, August 18). PEACE
TREATY OF WESTPHALIA. TyroCity.

Retrieved March 23, 2022, from
https://tyrocity.com/int-relations/peace-treaty-of-

Westphalia-

4gld#:%7E:text=The%201648%20Peace%20o
f%20Westphalia%20ended%20the%20Thi

rty,the%2

0principle%20that%20all%20sovereign%20sta
tes%20are%20equal.

[xxvii] Patton, S. (2019). The Peace of Westphalia and its
Affects on International Relations, Diplomacy

and Foreign Policy. The Histories, 10(1).

https://digitalcommons.lasalle.edu/cgi/viewcon
tent.cgi?article=1146&context=the_histories

[xxviii] Daudin, P. (2017, May 23). The Thirty Years'
War: The first modern war? Humanitarian Law &

Policy Blog. Retrieved March 23, 2022, from

https://blogs.icrc.org/law-and-
policy/2017/05/23/thirty-years-war-first-
modern

war/#:%7E:text=The%20Thirty%20Years'%2
0War%20is,by%20as%20much%20as%20

60%25.

[xxix] Patton, S. (2019). The Peace of Westphalia and it
Affects on International Relations, Diplomacy

and Foreign Policy. The Histories, 10(1).

https://digitalcommons.lasalle.edu/cgi/viewcontent.cgi?article=1146&context=the_histories

xxx Patton, S. (2019). The Peace of Westphalia and it Affects on International Relations, Diplomacy

and Foreign Policy. The Histories, 10(1).

https://digitalcommons.lasalle.edu/cgi/viewcontent.cgi?article=1146&context=the_histories

xxxi International Relations. (2013, August 18). PEACE TREATY OF WESTPHALIA. TyroCity.

Retrieved March 23, 2022, from https://tyrocity.com/int-relations/peace-treaty-of-

Westphalia-

4gld#:%7E.text=The%201648%20Peace%20of%20Westphalia%20ended%20the%20Thi

rty,the%2

0principle%20that%20all%20sovereign%20states%20are%20equal.

xxxii Patton, S. (2019). The Peace of Westphalia and it Affects on International Relations, Diplomacy

and Foreign Policy. The Histories, 10(1).

https://digitalcommons.lasalle.edu/cgi/viewcontent.cgi?article=1146&context=the_histories

[xxxiii] Patton, S. (2019). The Peace of Westphalia and it Affects on International Relations, Diplomacy

and Foreign Policy. The Histories, 10(1).

https://digitalcommons.lasalle.edu/cgi/viewcon tent.cgi?article=1146&context=the_histories

[xxxiv] Patton, S. (2019). The Peace of Westphalia and it Affects on International Relations, Diplomacy

and Foreign Policy. The Histories, 10(1).

https://digitalcommons.lasalle.edu/cgi/viewcon tent.cgi?article=1146&context=the_histories

[xxxv] Patton, S. (2019). The Peace of Westphalia and it Affects on International Relations, Diplomacy

and Foreign Policy. The Histories, 10(1).

https://digitalcommons.lasalle.edu/cgi/viewcon tent.cgi?article=1146&context=the_histories

[xxxvi] Bring, O. (2000). The Westphalian Peace Tradition in International Law From Jus ad Bellum to

Jus contra Bellum. International Law Study, 75(1). https://digital-

commons.usnwc.edu/cgi/viewcontent.cgi?artic le=1435&context=ils

[xxxvii] International Relations. (2013, August

179

18). PEACE TREATY OF WESTPHALIA. TyroCity.

Retrieved March 23, 2022, from
https://tyrocity.com/int-relations/peace-treaty-of-

Westphalia-

4gld#:%7E:text=The%201648%20Peace%20o
f%20Westphalia%20ended%20the%20Thi

rty,the%2

0principle%20that%20all%20sovereign%20sta
tes%20are%20equal.

[xxxviii] Beaulac, S. (2004). The Westphalian Model in
Defining International Law: Challenging the

Myth. Australian Journal of Legal
History, 8(2). http://www7.austlii.edu.au/cgi-

bin/viewdoc/au/journals/AJLH/2004/9.html#

[xxxix] Pharand, D. (1994). Perspectives on Sovereingty in
the Current Context: A Canadian

Viewpoint. Canada-United States Law
Journal, 20.

https://scholarlycommons.law.case.edu/cgi/vie
wcontent.cgi?referer=&httpsredir=1&article=2
0

05&context=cuslj

[xl] Beaulac, S. (2004). The Westphalian Model in Defining International Law: Challenging the

Myth. Australian Journal of Legal History, 8(2). http://www7.austlii.edu.au/cgi-

bin/viewdoc/au/journals/AJLH/2004/9.html#

[xli] Beaulac, S. (2004). The Westphalian Model in Defining International Law: Challenging the

Myth. Australian Journal of Legal History, 8(2). http://www7.austlii.edu.au/cgi-

bin/viewdoc/au/journals/AJLH/2004/9.html#

[xlii] International Relations. (2013, August 18). PEACE TREATY OF WESTPHALIA. TyroCity.

Retrieved March 23, 2022, from https://tyrocity.com/int-relations/peace-treaty-of-

Westphalia-

4gld#:%7E:text=The%201648%20Peace%20o f%20Westphalia%20ended%20the%20Thi

rty,the%2

0principle%20that%20all%20sovereign%20states%20 are%20equal.

[xliii] Zurbuchen, S. (2019). The Law of Nations and Natural Law, 1625–1800 (Vol. 1). Brill.

181

xliv International Relations. (2013, August 18). PEACE TREATY OF WESTPHALIA. TyroCity.

Retrieved March 23, 2022, from https://tyrocity.com/int-relations/peace-treaty-of-Westphalia-

4gld#:%7E:text=The%201648%20Peace%20of%20Westphalia%20ended%20the%20Thi

rty,the%2

0principle%20that%20all%20sovereign%20states%20are%20equal.

xlv Cameron, F. (2014, July 8). The Impact of the First World War and Its Implications for Europe Today | Heinrich Böll Stiftung. Heinrich-Böll-Stiftung. Retrieved April 5, 2022, from https://www.boell.de/en/2014/07/08/impact-first-world-war-and-its-implications-europe-today#Who%20caused%20the%20War?

xlvi Cameron, F. (2014, July 8). The Impact of the First World War and Its Implications for Europe Today | Heinrich Böll Stiftung. Heinrich-Böll-Stiftung. Retrieved April 5, 2022, from https://www.boell.de/en/2014/07/08/impact-first-world-war-and-its-implications-europe-today#Who%20caused%20the%20War?

xlvii Wisidagama, S. (2017, July 7). The Evolution of International Relations as a Field of Activity to

International Relations as an Academic Discipline. Academia. Retrieved April 5, 2022, from https://www.academia.edu/33799619/The_Evolution_o f_International_Relations_as_a_Field_of_Activity_to_ International_Relations_as_an_Academic_Discipline

[xlviii] Cameron, F. (2014, July 8). The Impact of the First World War and Its Implications for Europe Today | Heinrich Böll Stiftung. Heinrich-Böll-Stiftung. Retrieved April 5, 2022, from https://www.boell.de/en/2014/07/08/impact-first-world-war-and-its-implications-europe-today#Who%20caused%20the%20War?

[xlix] Cameron, F. (2014, July 8). The Impact of the First World War and Its Implications for Europe Today | Heinrich Böll Stiftung. Heinrich-Böll-Stiftung. Retrieved April 5, 2022, from https://www.boell.de/en/2014/07/08/impact-first-world-war-and-its-implications-europe-today#Who%20caused%20the%20War?

[l] Pfaltzgraff Jr., R. (2019). World War I and IR Theory. The Fletcher Forum of World Affairs, 43(1). https://www.jstor.org/stable/45289824

[li] Mock, G. (2018, November 8). How the Trauma and Struggles of World War I Helped Shape the Modern. Duke Today. Retrieved April 5, 2022, from https://today.duke.edu/2018/11/how-trauma-and-struggles-world-war-i-helped-shape-modern-world

[lii] Mock, G. (2018, November 8). How the Trauma and Struggles of World War I Helped Shape the Modern. Duke Today. Retrieved April 5, 2022, from https://today.duke.edu/2018/11/how-trauma-and-struggles-world-war-i-helped-shape-modern-world

[liii] Pfaltzgraff Jr., R. (2019). World War I and IR Theory. The Fletcher Forum of World Affairs, 43(1). https://www.jstor.org/stable/45289824

[liv] Pfaltzgraff Jr., R. (2019). World War I and IR Theory. The Fletcher Forum of World Affairs, 43(1). https://www.jstor.org/stable/45289824

[lv] Hindley, M. (2017). World War I Changed America and Transformed Its Role in International Relat. The National Endowment for the Humanities. Retrieved April 5, 2022, from https://www.neh.gov/humanities/2017/summer/feature/world-war-i-changed-america-and-transformed-its-role-in-international-relations

[lvi] Hindley, M. (2017). World War I Changed America and Transformed Its Role in International Relat. The National Endowment for the Humanities. Retrieved April 5, 2022, from https://www.neh.gov/humanities/2017/summer/feature/world-war-i-changed-america-and-transformed-its-role-in-international-relations

[lvii] Mock, G. (2018, November 8). How the Trauma and Struggles of World War I Helped Shape the

Modern. Duke Today. Retrieved April 5, 2022, from
https://today.duke.edu/2018/11/how-trauma-and-
struggles-world-war-i-helped-shape-modern-world

[lviii] Pfaltzgraff Jr., R. (2019). World War I and IR
Theory. The Fletcher Forum of World Affairs, 43(1).
https://www.jstor.org/stable/45289824

[lix] Pfaltzgraff Jr., R. (2019). World War I and IR
Theory. The Fletcher Forum of World Affairs, 43(1).
https://www.jstor.org/stable/45289824

[lx] Why is International Relations a discipline? (2019,
August 7). Nottingham Trent University Online.
Retrieved April 7, 2022, from
https://online.ntu.ac.uk/online-student-
experience/articles/international-relations-discipline-it-
important

[lxi] Why is International Relations a discipline? (2019,
August 7). Nottingham Trent University Online.
Retrieved April 7, 2022, from
https://online.ntu.ac.uk/online-student-
experience/articles/international-relations-discipline-it-
important

[lxii] Wisidagama, S. (2017, July 7). The Evolution of
International Relations as a Field of Activity to
International Relations as an Academic Discipline.
Academia. Retrieved April 7, 2022, from
https://www.academia.edu/33799619/The_Evolution_o
f_International_Relations_as_a_Field_of_Activity_to_

International_Relations_as_an_Academic_Discipline

[lxiii] Wisidagama, S. (2017, July 7). The Evolution of International Relations as a Field of Activity to International Relations as an Academic Discipline. Academia. Retrieved April 7, 2022, from https://www.academia.edu/33799619/The_Evolution_of_International_Relations_as_a_Field_of_Activity_to_International_Relations_as_an_Academic_Discipline

[lxiv] Wisidagama, S. (2017, July 7). The Evolution of International Relations as a Field of Activity to International Relations as an Academic Discipline. Academia. Retrieved April 7, 2022, from https://www.academia.edu/33799619/The_Evolution_of_International_Relations_as_a_Field_of_Activity_to_International_Relations_as_an_Academic_Discipline

[lxv] Wisidagama, S. (2017, July 7). The Evolution of International Relations as a Field of Activity to International Relations as an Academic Discipline. Academia. Retrieved April 7, 2022, from https://www.academia.edu/33799619/The_Evolution_of_International_Relations_as_a_Field_of_Activity_to_International_Relations_as_an_Academic_Discipline

[lxvi] The Cold War and its impact on international relations. (2021, May 27). iPleaders. Retrieved April 14, 2022, from https://blog.ipleaders.in/cold-war-impact-international-relations/

[lxvii] Naranjo, R. (2018, January 18). Historical analysis

186

of the Cold War. eHistory. Retrieved April 14, 2022, from https://ehistory.osu.edu/articles/historical-analysis-cold-war

[lxviii] The Cold War and its impact on international relations. (2021, May 27). iPleaders. Retrieved April 14, 2022, from https://blog.ipleaders.in/cold-war-impact-international-relations/

[lxix] The Cold War and its impact on international relations. (2021, May 27). iPleaders. Retrieved April 14, 2022, from https://blog.ipleaders.in/cold-war-impact-international-relations/

[lxx] Naranjo, R. (2018, January 18). Historical analysis of the Cold War. eHistory. Retrieved April 14, 2022, from https://ehistory.osu.edu/articles/historical-analysis-cold-war

[lxxi] The Cold War and its impact on international relations. (2021, May 27). iPleaders. Retrieved April 14, 2022, from https://blog.ipleaders.in/cold-war-impact-international-relations/

[lxxii] The Cold War: International Relations between 1945 and 1989 | Free Essay Example. (2020, September 4). StudyCorgi.Com. Retrieved April 14, 2022, from https://studycorgi.com/the-cold-war-international-relations-between-1945-and-1989/#:%7E:text=The%20Cold%20War%20significantly%20influenced%20the%20nature%20and,interest%20and%20the%20competition%20for%20nuclear%20s

upremacy.%20

[lxxiii] The Cold War and its impact on international relations. (2021, May 27). iPleaders. Retrieved April 14, 2022, from https://blog.ipleaders.in/cold-war-impact-international-relations/

[lxxiv] The Cold War and its impact on international relations. (2021, May 27). iPleaders. Retrieved April 14, 2022, from https://blog.ipleaders.in/cold-war-impact-international-relations/

[lxxv] The Cold War: International Relations between 1945 and 1989 | Free Essay Example. (2020, September 4). StudyCorgi.Com. Retrieved April 14, 2022, from https://studycorgi.com/the-cold-war-international-relations-between-1945-and-1989/#:%7E:text=The%20Cold%20War%20significan tly%20influenced%20the%20nature%20and,interest% 20and%20the%20competition%20for%20nuclear%20s upremacy.%20

[lxxvi] The Cold War: International Relations between 1945 and 1989 | Free Essay Example. (2020, September 4). StudyCorgi.Com. Retrieved April 14, 2022, from https://studycorgi.com/the-cold-war-international-relations-between-1945-and-1989/#:%7E:text=The%20Cold%20War%20significan tly%20influenced%20the%20nature%20and,interest% 20and%20the%20competition%20for%20nuclear%20s upremacy.%20

lxxvii The Cold War: International Relations between 1945 and 1989 | Free Essay Example. (2020, September 4). StudyCorgi.Com. Retrieved April 14, 2022, from https://studycorgi.com/the-cold-war-international-relations-between-1945-and-1989/#:%7E:text=The%20Cold%20War%20significan tly%20influenced%20the%20nature%20and,interest% 20and%20the%20competition%20for%20nuclear%20s upremacy.%20

lxxviii The Cold War and its impact on international relations. (2021, May 27). iPleaders. Retrieved April 14, 2022, from https://blog.ipleaders.in/cold-war-impact-international-relations/

lxxix Yilmaz, M. (2008). "The New World Order": An Outline of the Post-Cold War Era. Turkish Journal of International Relations, 7(4).

lxxx Roberts, A (2008). International Relations after the Cold War. International Affairs (Royal Institute of International Affairs 1944-), 84(2) , 335-350. http://www.jstor.org/stable/25144768

lxxxi Roberts, A (2008). International Relations after the Cold War. International Affairs (Royal Institute of International Affairs 1944-), 84(2) , 335-350. http://www.jstor.org/stable/25144768

lxxxii Matambo, E. (2020, April 22). International Relations Theory after the Cold War: China, the Global South and Non-state Actors. E-International Relations.

Retrieved April 14, 2022, from https://www.e-ir.info/2020/04/21/international-relations-theory-after-the-cold-war-china-the-global-south-and-non-state-actors/

lxxxiii Matambo, E. (2020, April 22). International Relations Theory after the Cold War: China, the Global South and Non-state Actors. E-International Relations. Retrieved April 14, 2022, from https://www.e-ir.info/2020/04/21/international-relations-theory-after-the-cold-war-china-the-global-south-and-non-state-actors/

lxxxiv Matambo, E. (2020, April 22). International Relations Theory after the Cold War: China, the Global South and Non-state Actors. E-International Relations. Retrieved April 14, 2022, from https://www.e-ir.info/2020/04/21/international-relations-theory-after-the-cold-war-china-the-global-south-and-non-state-actors/

lxxxv Sell, T. (Ed.). (2020). Post-Cold War International Relations. In A Primer on Politics. https://socialsci.libretexts.org/.

lxxxvi Chakravartty, A. (2017, June 12). *Scientific Realism (Stanford Encyclopedia of Philosophy)*. Stanford Encyclopedia of Philosophy. Retrieved June 1, 2022, from https://plato.stanford.edu/entries/scientific-realism/

lxxxvii Political Realism in International Relations

(Stanford Encyclopedia of Philosophy). (2017, May

24). Stanford Encyclopedia of Philosophy. Retrieved May 18, 2022, from

https://plato.stanford.edu/entries/realism-intl-relations/

[lxxxviii] Political Realism in International Relations (Stanford Encyclopedia of Philosophy). (2017, May

24). Stanford Encyclopedia of Philosophy. Retrieved May 18, 2022, from

https://plato.stanford.edu/entries/realism-intl-relations/

[lxxxix] Biswas, A. (n.d.). Realism Theory In International Relations In Detail. School of Political Science. Retrieved March 3, 2020, from https://schoolofpoliticalscience.com/realism-theory-in-international-relations/

[xc] Political Realism in International Relations (Stanford Encyclopedia of Philosophy). (2017, May

24). Stanford Encyclopedia of Philosophy. Retrieved May 18, 2022, from

https://plato.stanford.edu/entries/realism-intl-relations/

[xci] Political Realism in International Relations (Stanford Encyclopedia of Philosophy). (2017, May

24). Stanford Encyclopedia of Philosophy. Retrieved
  May 18, 2022, from

https://plato.stanford.edu/entries/realism-intl-relations/

xcii Biswas, A. (n.d.). Realism Theory In International
  Relations In Detail. School of Political Science.
  Retrieved May 18, 2020, from
  https://schoolofpoliticalscience.com/realism-
  theory-in-international-relations/

xciii Camisão, S. A. A. I. (2018, August 6). Introducing
  Realism in International Relations Theory. E-
  International Relations. Retrieved May 18,
  2022, from https://www.e-
  ir.info/2018/02/27/introducing-realism-in-
  international-relations-theory/

xciv Political Realism in International Relations
  (Stanford Encyclopedia of Philosophy). (2017,
  May

24). Stanford Encyclopedia of Philosophy. Retrieved
  May 18, 2022, from

https://plato.stanford.edu/entries/realism-intl-relations/

xcv Political Realism in International Relations
  (Stanford Encyclopedia of Philosophy). (2017,
  May

24). Stanford Encyclopedia of Philosophy. Retrieved
  May 18, 2022, from

https://plato.stanford.edu/entries/realism-intl-relations/

[xcvi] Political Realism in International Relations (Stanford Encyclopedia of Philosophy). (2017, May

24). Stanford Encyclopedia of Philosophy. Retrieved May 18, 2022, from

https://plato.stanford.edu/entries/realism-intl-relations/

[xcvii] Political Realism in International Relations (Stanford Encyclopedia of Philosophy). (2017, May

24). Stanford Encyclopedia of Philosophy. Retrieved May 18, 2022, from

https://plato.stanford.edu/entries/realism-intl-relations/

[xcviii] Political Realism in International Relations (Stanford Encyclopedia of Philosophy). (2017, May

24). Stanford Encyclopedia of Philosophy. Retrieved May 18, 2022, from

https://plato.stanford.edu/entries/realism-intl-relations/

[xcix] Biswas, A. (n.d.). Realism Theory In International Relations In Detail. School of Political Science. Retrieved May 18, 2020, from https://schoolofpoliticalscience.com/realism-theory-in-international-relations/

[c] Political Realism in International Relations (Stanford Encyclopedia of Philosophy). (2017, May

24). Stanford Encyclopedia of Philosophy. Retrieved May 18, 2022, from

https://plato.stanford.edu/entries/realism-intl-relations/

[ci] Political Realism in International Relations (Stanford Encyclopedia of Philosophy). (2017, May

24). Stanford Encyclopedia of Philosophy. Retrieved May 18, 2022, from

https://plato.stanford.edu/entries/realism-intl-relations

[cii] Political Realism in International Relations (Stanford Encyclopedia of Philosophy). (2017, May

24). Stanford Encyclopedia of Philosophy. Retrieved May 18, 2022, from

https://plato.stanford.edu/entries/realism-intl-relations

[ciii] Political Realism in International Relations (Stanford Encyclopedia of Philosophy). (2017, May

24). Stanford Encyclopedia of Philosophy. Retrieved May 18, 2022, from

https://plato.stanford.edu/entries/realism-intl-relations

[civ] Biswas, A. (n.d.). Realism Theory In International

Relations In Detail. School of Political Science. Retrieved May 18, 2020, from https://schoolofpoliticalscience.com/realism-theory-in-international-relations/

cv Biswas, A. (n.d.). Realism Theory In International Relations In Detail. School of Political Science. Retrieved May 18, 2020, from https://schoolofpoliticalscience.com/realism-theory-in-international-relations/

cvi Political Realism in International Relations (Stanford Encyclopedia of Philosophy). (2017, May

24). Stanford Encyclopedia of Philosophy. Retrieved May 18, 2022, from

https://plato.stanford.edu/entries/realism-intl-relations

cvii Political Realism in International Relations (Stanford Encyclopedia of Philosophy). (2017, May

24). Stanford Encyclopedia of Philosophy. Retrieved May 18, 2022, from

https://plato.stanford.edu/entries/realism-intl-relations

cviii Biswas, A. (n.d.). Realism Theory In International Relations In Detail. School of Political Science. Retrieved May 18, 2020, from https://schoolofpoliticalscience.com/realism-theory-in-

international-relations/

cix Political Realism in International Relations
(Stanford Encyclopedia of Philosophy). (2017,
May

24). Stanford Encyclopedia of Philosophy. Retrieved
May 18, 2022, from

https://plato.stanford.edu/entries/realism-intl-relations

cx Lobell, S. E. (2010, March 1). *Structural
Realism/Offensive and Defensive Realism.*
Oxford University Press. Retrieved June 1,
2022, from
https://oxfordre.com/internationalstudies/view/
10.1093/acrefore/9780190846626.001.0001/ac
refore-9780190846626-e-304

cxi Biswas, A. (n.d.) Realism Theory In International
Relations In Detail. School of Political
Science. Retrieved May 18, 2020, from
https://schoolofpoliticalscience.com/realism-
theory-in-international-relations/

cxii Jeffrey W. Meiser. (2018, February 18). Introducing
Liberalism in International Relations Theory. E-
International Relations. Retrieved April 16,
2022, from https://www.e-
ir.info/2018/02/18/introducing-liberalism-in-
international-relations-theory/

cxiii Jeffrey W. Meiser. (2018, February 18).

196

Introducing Liberalism in International Relations Theory. E-International Relations. Retrieved April 16, 2022, from https://www.e-ir.info/2018/02/18/introducing-liberalism-in-international-relations-theory/

cxiv BINU JOSEPH. (n.d.). Liberalism: A Brief Understanding of Liberal Theory in International Relations. Https://Www.Academia.Edu/. Retrieved April 16, 2022, from https://www.academia.edu/37173609/LIBERAL ISM_A_Brief_Understanding_of_Liberal_Theor y_in_International_Relations

cxv Lerner, M. (n.d.). *liberalism - Classical liberalism*. Encyclopedia Britannica. Retrieved June 1, 2022, from https://www.britannica.com/topic/liberalism/Cl assical-liberalism

cxvi BINU JOSEPH. (n.d.). Liberalism: A Brief Understanding of Liberal Theory in International Relations. Https://Www.Academia.Edu/. Retrieved April 16, 2022, from https://www.academia.edu/37173609/LIBERAL ISM_A_Brief_Understanding_of_Liberal_Theor y_in_International_Relations

cxvii BINU JOSEPH. (n.d.). Liberalism: A Brief Understanding of Liberal Theory in International Relations. Https://Www.Academia.Edu/. Retrieved April 16, 2022, from

https://www.academia.edu/37173609/LIBERAL
ISM_A_Brief_Understanding_of_Liberal_Theor
y_in_International_Relations

[cxviii] Jeffrey W. Meiser. (2018, February 18).
Introducing Liberalism in International Relations
Theory. E-International Relations. Retrieved
April 16, 2022, from https://www.e-
ir.info/2018/02/18/introducing-liberalism-in-
international-relations-theory/

[cxix] BINU JOSEPH. (n.d.). Liberalism: A Brief
Understanding of Liberal Theory in International
Relations. Https://Www.Academia.Edu/.
Retrieved April 16, 2022, from
https://www.academia.edu/37173609/LIBERAL
ISM_A_Brief_Understanding_of_Liberal_Theor
y_in_International_Relations

[cxx] Andrew Moravcsik. (n.d.). Liberalism and
International Relations Theory. Princeton.Edu.
Retrieved April 16, 2022, from
https://www.princeton.edu/~amoravcs/library/lib
eralism_working.pdf

[cxxi] Jeffrey W. Meiser. (2018, February 18).
Introducing Liberalism in International Relations
Theory. E-International Relations. Retrieved
April 16, 2022, from https://www.e-
ir.info/2018/02/18/introducing-liberalism-in-
international-relations-theory/

cxxii Jeffrey W. Meiser. (2018, February 18). Introducing Liberalism in International Relations Theory. E-International Relations. Retrieved April 16, 2022, from https://www.e-ir.info/2018/02/18/introducing-liberalism-in-international-relations-theory/

cxxiii Jeffrey W. Meiser. (2018, February 18). Introducing Liberalism in International Relations Theory. E-International Relations. Retrieved April 16, 2022, from https://www.e-ir.info/2018/02/18/introducing-liberalism-in-international-relations-theory/

cxxiv BINU JOSEPH. (n.d.). Liberalism: A Brief Understanding of Liberal Theory in International Relations. Https://Www.Academia.Edu/. Retrieved April 16, 2022, from https://www.academia.edu/37173609/LIBERAL ISM_A_Brief_Understanding_of_Liberal_Theor y_in_International_Relations

cxxv BINU JOSEPH. (n.d.). Liberalism: A Brief Understanding of Liberal Theory in International Relations. Https://Www.Academia.Edu/. Retrieved April 16, 2022, from https://www.academia.edu/37173609/LIBERAL ISM_A_Brief_Understanding_of_Liberal_Theor y_in_International_Relations

cxxvi Andrew Moravcsik. (n.d.). Liberalism and International Relations Theory. Princeton.Edu.

Retrieved April 16, 2022, from
https://www.princeton.edu/~amoravcs/library/lib
eralism_working.pdf

[cxxvii] BINU JOSEPH. (n.d.). Liberalism: A Brief
Understanding of Liberal Theory in International
Relations. Https://Www.Academia.Edu/.
Retrieved April 16, 2022, from
https://www.academia.edu/37173609/LIBERAL
ISM_A_Brief_Understanding_of_Liberal_Theor
y_in_International_Relations

[cxxviii] BINU JOSEPH. (n.d.). Liberalism: A Brief
Understanding of Liberal Theory in International
Relations. Https://Www.Academia.Edu/.
Retrieved April 16, 2022, from
https://www.academia.edu/37173609/LIBERAL
ISM_A_Brief_Understanding_of_Liberal_Theor
y_in_International_Relations

[cxxix] BINU JOSEPH. (n.d.). Liberalism: A Brief
Understanding of Liberal Theory in International
Relations. Https://Www.Academia.Edu/.
Retrieved April 16, 2022, from
https://www.academia.edu/37173609/LIBERAL
ISM_A_Brief_Understanding_of_Liberal_Theor
y_in_International_Relations

[cxxx] BINU JOSEPH. (n.d.). Liberalism: A Brief
Understanding of Liberal Theory in International
Relations. Https://Www.Academia.Edu/.
Retrieved April 16, 2022, from

https://www.academia.edu/37173609/LIBERAL
ISM_A_Brief_Understanding_of_Liberal_Theor
y_in_International_Relations

cxxxi BINU JOSEPH. (n.d.). Liberalism: A Brief
Understanding of Liberal Theory in International
Relations. Https://Www.Academia.Edu/.
Retrieved April 16, 2022, from
https://www.academia.edu/37173609/LIBERAL
ISM_A_Brief_Understanding_of_Liberal_Theor
y_in_International_Relations

cxxxii Moravcsik, A. (2011, July). *The New Liberalism.*
The Oxford Handbook of Political Science.
Retrieved June 3, 2022, from
https://www.oxfordhandbooks.com/view/10.10
93/oxfordhb/9780199604456.001.0001/oxford
hb-9780199604456-e-033

cxxxiii Sarina Theys. (2018, April 23). Introducing
Constructivism in International Relations
Theory. E-International Relations. Retrieved
April 16, 2022, from https://www.e-
ir.info/2018/02/23/introducing-constructivism-
in-international-relations-theory/

cxxxiv Sarina Theys. (2018, April 23). Introducing
Constructivism in International Relations Theory. E-
International Relations. Retrieved April 16, 2022, from
https://www.e-ir.info/2018/02/23/introducing-
constructivism-in-international-relations-theory/

cxxxv Sarina Theys. (2018, April 23). Introducing

Constructivism in International Relations
Theory. E-International Relations. Retrieved
April 16, 2022, from https://www.e-
ir.info/2018/02/23/introducing-constructivism-
in-international-relations-theory/

cxxxvi Sarina Theys. (2018, April 23). Introducing
Constructivism in International Relations
Theory. E-International Relations. Retrieved
April 16, 2022, from https://www.e-
ir.info/2018/02/23/introducing-constructivism-
in-international-relations-theory/

cxxxvii Constructivism in International Relations. (n.d.).
International Affairs Forum. Retrieved April 16,
2022, from https://www.ia-
forum.org/Content/ViewInternal_Document.cfm
?contenttype_id=5&ContentID=8773

cxxxviii Faqi Ahmad. (2020, October 11). The Theory of
Constructivism in International Relations.
Https://Www.Academia.Edu/. Retrieved April
16, 2022, from
https://www.academia.edu/44540969/The_Theor
y_of_Constructivism_in_International_Relations

cxxxix Sarina Theys. (2018, April 23). Introducing
Constructivism in International Relations
Theory. E-International Relations. Retrieved
April 16, 2022, from https://www.e-
ir.info/2018/02/23/introducing-constructivism-
in-international-relations-theory/

[cxl] Sarina Theys. (2018, April 23). Introducing Constructivism in International Relations Theory. E-International Relations. Retrieved April 16, 2022, from https://www.e-ir.info/2018/02/23/introducing-constructivism-in-international-relations-theory/

[cxli] Sarina Theys. (2018, April 23). Introducing Constructivism in International Relations Theory. E-International Relations. Retrieved April 16, 2022, from https://www.e-ir.info/2018/02/23/introducing-constructivism-in-international-relations-theory/

[cxlii] Faqi Ahmad. (2020, October 11). The Theory of Constructivism in International Relations. Https://Www.Academia.Edu/. Retrieved April 16, 2022, from https://www.academia.edu/44540969/The_Theory_of_Constructivism_in_International_Relations

[cxliii] Faqi Ahmad. (2020, October 11). The Theory of Constructivism in International Relations. Https://Www.Academia.Edu/. Retrieved April 16, 2022, from https://www.academia.edu/44540969/The_Theory_of_Constructivism_in_International_Relations

[cxliv] Constructivism in International Relations. (n.d.). International Affairs Forum. Retrieved April 16, 2022, from https://www.ia-forum.org/Content/ViewInternal_Document.cfm

?contenttype_id=5&ContentID=8773

cxlv Emanuel Adler. (2002). Constructivism and
International Relations.
Https://Omnilogos.Com/. Retrieved April 16,
2022, from
https://omnilogos.com/constructivism-and-
international-relations/

cxlvi Constructivism in International Relations. (n.d.).
International Affairs Forum. Retrieved April 16,
2022, from https://www.ia-
forum.org/Content/ViewInternal_Document.cfm
?contenttype_id=5&ContentID=8773

cxlvii Sarina Theys. (2018, April 23). Introducing
Constructivism in International Relations
Theory. E-International Relations. Retrieved
April 16, 2022, from https://www.e-
ir.info/2018/02/23/introducing-constructivism-
in-international-relations-theory/

cxlviii Sarina Theys. (2018, April 23). Introducing
Constructivism in International Relations
Theory. E-International Relations. Retrieved
April 16, 2022, from https://www.e-
ir.info/2018/02/23/introducing-constructivism-
in-international-relations-theory/

cxlix Emanuel Adler. (2002). Constructivism and
International Relations.
Https://Omnilogos.Com/. Retrieved April 16,

2022, from
https://omnilogos.com/constructivism-and-international-relations/

cl Emanuel Adler. (2002). Constructivism and International Relations. Https://Omnilogos.Com/. Retrieved April 16, 2022, from https://omnilogos.com/constructivism-and-international-relations/

cli Constructivism in International Relations. (n.d.). International Affairs Forum. Retrieved April 16, 2022, from https://www.ia-forum.org/Content/ViewInternal_Document.cfm?contenttype_id=5&ContentID=8773

clii Emanuel Adler. (2002). Constructivism and International Relations. Https://Omnilogos.Com/. Retrieved April 16, 2022, from https://omnilogos.com/constructivism-and-international-relations/

cliii Emanuel Adler. (2002). Constructivism and International Relations. Https://Omnilogos.Com/. Retrieved April 16, 2022, from https://omnilogos.com/constructivism-and-international-relations/

cliv Emanuel Adler. (2002). Constructivism and

International Relations.
Https://Omnilogos.Com/. Retrieved April 16,
2022, from
https://omnilogos.com/constructivism-and-
international-relations/

[clv] Faqi Ahmad. (2020, October 11). The Theory of
Constructivism in International Relations.
Https://Www.Academia.Edu/. Retrieved April
16, 2022, from
https://www.academia.edu/44540969/The_Theor
y_of_Constructivism_in_International_Relations

[clvi] Emanuel Adler. (2002). Constructivism and
International Relations.
Https://Omnilogos.Com/. Retrieved April 16,
2022, from
https://omnilogos.com/constructivism-and-
international-relations/

[clvii] Emanuel Adler. (2002). Constructivism and
International Relations.
Https://Omnilogos.Com/. Retrieved April 16,
2022, from
https://omnilogos.com/constructivism-and-
international-relations/

[clviii] Faqi Ahmad. (2020, October 11). The Theory of
Constructivism in International Relations.
Https://Www.Academia.Edu/. Retrieved April
16, 2022, from
https://www.academia.edu/44540969/The_Theor

y_of_Constructivism_in_International_Relations

clix Faqi Ahmad. (2020, October 11). The Theory of
    Constructivism in International Relations.
    Https://Www.Academia.Edu/. Retrieved April
    16, 2022, from
    https://www.academia.edu/44540969/The_Theor
    y_of_Constructivism_in_International_Relations

clx Faqi Ahmad. (2020, October 11). The Theory of
    Constructivism in International Relations.
    Https://Www.Academia.Edu/. Retrieved April
    16, 2022, from
    https://www.academia.edu/44540969/The_Theor
    y_of_Constructivism_in_International_Relations

clxi Emanuel Adler. (2002). Constructivism and
    International Relations.
    Https://Omnilogos.Com/. Retrieved April 16,
    2022, from
    https://omnilogos.com/constructivism-and-
    international-relations/

clxii Maïa Pal. (2018, February 25). Introducing
    Marxism in International Relations Theory. E-
    International Relations. Retrieved April 16,
    2022, from https://www.e-
    ir.info/2018/02/25/introducing-marxism-in-
    international-relations-theory/

clxiii Campbell, S. L. (2018, June 26). *The Differences
    Between Marxism, Socialism & Communism.*

Classroom.Synonym. Retrieved June 4, 2022, from https://classroom.synonym.com/differences-between-marxism-socialism-communism-17064.html

clxiv To-retro Blog. (2018, September 30). *Közveszélyes munkakerülés - ma már nevetségesnek tűnik, régen simán börtön járt érte | szmo.hu.* Szeretlek Magyarország. Retrieved June 4, 2022, from https://www.szeretlekmagyarorszag.hu/multun k/kozveszelyes-munkakerules-ma-mar-nevetsegesnek-tunik-regen-siman-borton-jart-erte/

clxv Campbell, S. L. (2018, June 26). *The Differences Between Marxism, Socialism & Communism.* Classroom.Synonym. Retrieved June 4, 2022, from https://classroom.synonym.com/differences-between-marxism-socialism-communism-17064.html

clxvi Campbell, S. L. (2018, June 26). *The Differences Between Marxism, Socialism & Communism.* Classroom.Synonym. Retrieved June 4, 2022, from https://classroom.synonym.com/differences-between-marxism-socialism-communism-17064.html

clxvii Campbell, S. L. (2018, June 26). *The Differences Between Marxism, Socialism & Communism.*

Classroom.Synonym. Retrieved June 4, 2022, from https://classroom.synonym.com/differences-between-marxism-socialism-communism-17064.html

clxviii Ankit Tomar. (n.d.). Theories of International Relations and World History. Http://Dcac.Du.Ac.In/. Retrieved April 16, 2022, from http://dcac.du.ac.in/documents/E-Resource/2020/Metrial/410MukeshBagorial.pdf

clxix Maïa Pal. (2018, February 25). Introducing Marxism in International Relations Theory. E-International Relations. Retrieved April 16, 2022, from https://www.e-ir.info/2018/02/25/introducing-marxism-in-international-relations-theory/

clxx Maïa Pal. (2018, February 25). Introducing Marxism in International Relations Theory. E-International Relations. Retrieved April 16, 2022, from https://www.e-ir.info/2018/02/25/introducing-marxism-in-international-relations-theory/

clxxi Ankit Tomar. (n.d.). *Theories of International Relations and World History.* Http://Dcac.Du.Ac.In/. Retrieved April 16, 2022, from http://dcac.du.ac.in/documents/E-Resource/2020/Metrial/410MukeshBagorial.pdf

clxxii Maïa Pal. (2018, February 25). Introducing

Marxism in International Relations Theory. E-
International Relations. Retrieved April 16,
2022, from https://www.e-
ir.info/2018/02/25/introducing-marxism-in-
international-relations-theory/

clxxiii Ankit Tomar. (n.d.). *Theories of International
Relations and World History*.
Http://Dcac.Du.Ac.In/. Retrieved April 16, 2022,
from http://dcac.du.ac.in/documents/E-
Resource/2020/Metrial/410MukeshBagorial.pdf

clxxiv Maïa Pal. (2018, February 25). Introducing
Marxism in International Relations Theory. E-
International Relations. Retrieved April 16,
2022, from https://www.e-
ir.info/2018/02/25/introducing-marxism-in-
international-relations-theory/

clxxv Ankit Tomar. (n.d.). *Theories of International
Relations and World History*.
Http://Dcac.Du.Ac.In/. Retrieved April 16, 2022,
from http://dcac.du.ac.in/documents/E-
Resource/2020/Metrial/410MukeshBagorial.pdf

clxxvi Ankit Tomar. (n.d.). *Theories of International
Relations and World History*.
Http://Dcac.Du.Ac.In/. Retrieved April 16, 2022,
from http://dcac.du.ac.in/documents/E-
Resource/2020/Metrial/410MukeshBagorial.pdf

clxxvii Ankit Tomar. (n.d.). *Theories of International*

Relations and World History.
Http://Dcac.Du.Ac.In/. Retrieved April 16, 2022,
from http://dcac.du.ac.in/documents/E-
Resource/2020/Metrial/410MukeshBagoria1.pdf

clxxviii Ankit Tomar. (n.d.). Theories of International
Relations and World History.
Http://Dcac.Du.Ac.In/. Retrieved April 16, 2022,
from http://dcac.du.ac.in/documents/E-
Resource/2020/Metrial/410MukeshBagoria1.pdf

clxxix Maïa Pal. (2018, February 25). Introducing
Marxism in International Relations Theory. E-
International Relations. Retrieved April 16,
2022, from https://www.e-
ir.info/2018/02/25/introducing-marxism-in-
international-relations-theory/

clxxx Maïa Pal. (2018, February 25). Introducing
Marxism in International Relations Theory. E-
International Relations. Retrieved April 16,
2022, from https://www.e-
ir.info/2018/02/25/introducing-marxism-in-
international-relations-theory/

clxxxi Ankit Tomar. (n.d.). Theories of International
Relations and World History.
Http://Dcac.Du.Ac.In/. Retrieved April 16, 2022,
from http://dcac.du.ac.in/documents/E-
Resource/2020/Metrial/410MukeshBagoria1.pdf

clxxxii Maïa Pal. (2018, February 25). Introducing

Marxism in International Relations Theory. E-
International Relations. Retrieved April 16,
2022, from https://www.e-
ir.info/2018/02/25/introducing-marxism-in-
international-relations-theory/

clxxxiii Ankit Tomar. (n.d.). Theories of International
Relations and World History.
Http://Dcac.Du.Ac.In/. Retrieved April 16, 2022,
from http://dcac.du.ac.in/documents/E-
Resource/2020/Metrial/410MukeshBagoria1.pdf

clxxxiv Ankit Tomar. (n.d.). *Theories of International
Relations and World History.*
Http://Dcac.Du.Ac.In/. Retrieved April 16, 2022,
from http://dcac.du.ac.in/documents/E-
Resource/2020/Metrial/410MukeshBagoria1.pdf

clxxxv Ankit Tomar. (n.d.). *Theories of International
Relations and World History.*
Http://Dcac.Du.Ac.In/. Retrieved April 16, 2022,
from http://dcac.du.ac.in/documents/E-
Resource/2020/Metrial/410MukeshBagoria1.pdf

clxxxvi Ankit Tomar. (n.d.). Theories of International
Relations and World History.
Http://Dcac.Du.Ac.In/. Retrieved April 16, 2022,
from http://dcac.du.ac.in/documents/E-
Resource/2020/Metrial/410MukeshBagoria1.pdf

clxxxvii Maïa Pal. (2018, February 25). Introducing
Marxism in International Relations Theory. E-

212

International Relations. Retrieved April 16, 2022, from https://www.e-ir.info/2018/02/25/introducing-marxism-in-international-relations-theory/

clxxxviii Ankit Tomar. (n.d.). Theories of International Relations and World History. Http://Dcac.Du.Ac.In/. Retrieved April 16, 2022, from http://dcac.du.ac.in/documents/E-Resource/2020/Metrial/410MukeshBagoria1.pdf

clxxxix Sarah Smith. (2018, January 4). Introducing Feminism in International Relations Theory. E-International Relations. Retrieved April 16, 2022, from https://www.e-ir.info/2018/01/04/feminism-in-international-relations-theory/

cxc Sarah Smith. (2018, January 4). Introducing Feminism in International Relations Theory. E-International Relations. Retrieved April 16, 2022, from https://www.e-ir.info/2018/01/04/feminism-in-international-relations-theory/

cxci Ariella, S. (2022, April 21). *25 Women In Leadership Statistics [2022]: Facts On The Gender Gap In Corporate And Political Leadership – Zippia*. Zippier. Retrieved June 4, 2022, from https://www.zippia.com/advice/women-in-leadership-statistics/

213

[cxcii] Jacqui True. (2017, February 30). Feminism and Gender Studies in International Relations Theory. Oxford Research Encyclopedia of International Studies. Retrieved April 16, 2022, from https://oxfordre.com/internationalstudies/view/10.1093/acrefore/9780190846626.001.0001/acrefore-9780190846626-e-46

[cxciii] Lianboi Vaiphei. (n.d.). Feminist Perspectives and International Relations. Http://Dcac.Du.Ac.In/. Retrieved April 16, 2022, from http://dcac.du.ac.in/documents/E-Resource/2020/Metrial/409MukeshBagoria2.pdf

[cxciv] Bjork, P. (2021, March 4). *A Brief Look at the Four Waves of Feminism*. TheHumanist.Com. Retrieved June 5, 2022, from https://thehumanist.com/commentary/a-brief-look-at-the-four-waves-of-feminism/

[cxcv] Jacqui True. (2017, February 30). Feminism and Gender Studies in International Relations Theory. Oxford Research Encyclopedia of International Studies. Retrieved April 16, 2022, from https://oxfordre.com/internationalstudies/view/10.1093/acrefore/9780190846626.001.0001/acrefore-9780190846626-e-46

[cxcvi] Lianboi Vaiphei. (n.d.). Feminist Perspectives and International Relations. Http://Dcac.Du.Ac.In/.

Retrieved April 16, 2022, from
http://dcac.du.ac.in/documents/E-
Resource/2020/Metrial/409MukeshBagoria2.pdf

[cxcvii] Lianboi Vaiphei. (n.d.). Feminist Perspectives and
International Relations. Http://Dcac.Du.Ac.In/.
Retrieved April 16, 2022, from
http://dcac.du.ac.in/documents/E-
Resource/2020/Metrial/409MukeshBagoria2.pdf

[cxcviii] Lianboi Vaiphei. (n.d.). Feminist Perspectives and
International Relations. Http://Dcac.Du.Ac.In/.
Retrieved April 16, 2022, from
http://dcac.du.ac.in/documents/E-
Resource/2020/Metrial/409MukeshBagoria2.pdf

[cxcix] Lianboi Vaiphei. (n.d.). Feminist Perspectives and
International Relations. Http://Dcac.Du.Ac.In/.
Retrieved April 16, 2022, from
http://dcac.du.ac.in/documents/E-
Resource/2020/Metrial/409MukeshBagoria2.pdf

[cc] Lianboi Vaiphei. (n.d.). Feminist Perspectives and
International Relations. Http://Dcac.Du.Ac.In/.
Retrieved April 16, 2022, from
http://dcac.du.ac.in/documents/E-
Resource/2020/Metrial/409MukeshBagoria2.pdf

[cci] Jacqui True. (2017, February 30). Feminism and
Gender Studies in International Relations
Theory. Oxford Research Encyclopedia of
International Studies. Retrieved April 16, 2022,

from
https://oxfordre.com/internationalstudies/view/1
0.1093/acrefore/9780190846626.001.0001/acref
ore-9780190846626-e-46

[ccii] Lianboi Vaiphei. (n.d.). Feminist Perspectives and
International Relations. Http://Dcac.Du.Ac.In/.
Retrieved April 16, 2022, from
http://dcac.du.ac.in/documents/E-
Resource/2020/Metrial/409MukeshBagoria2.pdf

[cciii] Lianboi Vaiphei. (n.d.). Feminist Perspectives and
International Relations. Http://Dcac.Du.Ac.In/.
Retrieved April 16, 2022, from
http://dcac.du.ac.in/documents/E-
Resource/2020/Metrial/409MukeshBagoria2.pdf

[cciv] Lianboi Vaiphei. (n.d.). Feminist Perspectives and
International Relations. Http://Dcac.Du.Ac.In/.
Retrieved April 16, 2022, from
http://dcac.du.ac.in/documents/E-
Resource/2020/Metrial/409MukeshBagoria2.pdf

[ccv] Lianboi Vaiphei. (n.d.). Feminist Perspectives and
International Relations. Http://Dcac.Du.Ac.In/.
Retrieved April 16, 2022, from
http://dcac.du.ac.in/documents/E-
Resource/2020/Metrial/409MukeshBagoria2.pdf

[ccvi] Lianboi Vaiphei. (n.d.). Feminist Perspectives and
International Relations. Http://Dcac.Du.Ac.In/.
Retrieved April 16, 2022, from

http://dcac.du.ac.in/documents/E-Resource/2020/Metrial/409MukeshBagoria2.pdf

Made in the USA
Las Vegas, NV
26 November 2024

12676293R00125